SLOW TAKES
A LONG TIME

SLOW TAKES A LONG TIME

A 'SPECIAL' ORPHAN'S MEDITATION ON LOVE AND APPRECIATION

LESLI HICKS

RESOURCE *Publications* • Eugene, Oregon

Resource Publications
A division of Wipf and Stock Publishers
199 W 8th Ave, Suite 3
Eugene, OR 97401

Slow Takes a Long Time
A 'Special' Orphan's Meditation on Love and Appreciation
By Hicks, Lesli
Copyright © 2016 by Hicks, Lesli All rights reserved.
Softcover ISBN-13: 978-1-7252-9177-5
Hardcover ISBN-13: 978-1-7252-9176-8
eBook ISBN-13: 978-1-7252-9178-2
Publication date 11/9/2020
Previously published by Tate Publishing, 2016

This edition is a scanned facsimile of the original edition published in 2016.

To Steve, a George Bailey who has made this a wonderful life

Acknowledgements

I cannot identify the many great educators who have supported our son without identifying him. Suffice it to say that there have been many, including two of his teachers in China, who bid the little boy named Guo farewell in late July 2008, giving him an empty old camera and encouraging him to explore the hotel. Perhaps more importantly, they told him we were "good" in those very first minutes of the handoff; and he nodded, saying he wanted to come with us. He has been with us ever since.

To his second first-grade teacher, who said at the time, "I see him as any *normal* first grader." Thank you for giving us encouragement and sending him a note when you too journeyed to China after he was no longer in your class. Remember that during the holiday break, he cried for you. He missed you. And you still sent him notes even as he finished second grade. While you did not know it, your earlier kindness grounded our unease when subsequent reports were not so encouraging.

To our friends Molly O'Regan and Jeanette Williamson, who have welcomed our son into their lives and reassured us that he has unique gifts, including an infectious smile. One of you is an educator, and the other of you lovingly tended to our daughter in your in-home day care then encouraged us when our families got together for pizza (one of his favorite foods starting with the first time we ordered it at room service in China). Mothers yourselves, your observations have meant the world in our world. You have become his American *aunts*.

To the O'Regan and Williamson children, who sometimes have been like our own, for their unofficial inclusion therapy.

To our friends Mike Francis, Mike McCrary, Greg Shilts, Bob Mansfield, Ian O'Regan (a published mystery writer), Johnny Williamson, and Tim White, who have provided my son's father with the respite of talk about sports, especially football and baseball or actual golf games.

To Robert and Laura Centeno, who introduced our son to scouting and the responsibilities of camp.

To our friend, "Aunt" Sharon Garant, who has been another sister and mother, supporting not only our daughter and son but us when we were especially worried about the use of the term *mentally retarded* (MR). She has provided the respite of listening.

To friends Martha Mitchell and Peggy Mayfield, former colleagues from Corporate America who are part of the "ladies who lunch" and inspire so much laughter, along with insights into what matters.

To our friend Peggy Martinez, who has babysat (one of the few our son trusts enough to remain with) and, more importantly, spent time talking and listening to our children—and us. She too has a "book" in her of survival dating back to childhood. Our son asked if she is his "aunt or grandmother." She has been both and beyond.

To our friend "Uncle" Tom Honeycutt, who has held our children upside down until they giggled themselves nearly out of breath.

To Randy and Annabelle Trusty, who—with their daughter, Chloe (our daughter's orphanage mate), and biological son, Jackson—have been fun friends and vacation partners, be the venue a theme park or a Lone Star State beach.

To our friend and lawyer, Richard Noll, who has advised on us on wills and guardians; and his wife, Diane Abdo, who, with Rick, is a role model in university-level teaching and friendship.

To Jeffrey Michel, a young man who is one of our son's best friends, for coming over for sleepovers and hikes, teaching friendship at the elementary-school level. He never has made our son feel like a weird kid.

To our social worker, Mara Hudock, who has provided gentle guidance and resources longer after the year-end report was due.

To our family's "Uncle Bob" Johnsmiller, who has been a great-godfather and quasi grandfather to both our children and a life coach in parenting. To his late wife, Marilynn, a mother of five children in the 1940s and 1950s, who made our son a cup with the letter G on it months before she died, when we believed he would be an adopted girl we would call Grace.

To our dentist, Dr. Ernst Schelb and his wife, Rita, who have helped us determine our son's chronological age and patiently taught him to brush.

To Dr. James Wicoff, who has been a brilliant diagnostician and support for our family, especially with our two adoptions spanning more than ten years.

To the department deans, chairpeople, department heads, and colleagues where I teach history, for supporting me as a budding lecturer.

To my husband's company's management team and colleagues, who have supported this working father who now and then has needed to handle bus pickups, doctor's appointments, and school meetings. They always greet our son warmly.

To multiple students who have met my children and commented on the miracles they are and said they too might adopt a child in search of family someday.

To our wonderful neighbors, who have welcomed this *curious* Chinese boy into our 'hood, playing games with him or waiting at the bus stop when we are late.

Contents

February 2012 13
Old Life, New Parents 23
Old House, New Life 37
A List of My Favorite Things 43
Special Education 51
In America Now 59
Meaning of Life 65
Alphabet Soup 77
Find My Bliss 81
Love in Any Language 89
Counting the Length of a Hug 93
Lessons from the Happiest Boy in the World 105
Lessons I have Taught My Family 109
Backword 115
Appendix 127

February 2012

Somewhere in Texas

I am retarded.

Oh no, that wasn't the exact word she used. *Intellectually disabled* or *intellectually delayed* or *ID* is the term today, after all.

After a series of e-mail and text messages, one of the "experts" at my public school told my mother in person that the ID label today is what Mom's generation referred to as *mentally retarded*—her exact words.

Some people, even other students, still call it MR. *Everybody* knows that.

The sincere lady, in a neutral-colored sweater set and complementary necklace, thought the MR reference would help Mom better understand the implications of the description. Well, it sure did help clear things up—or maybe it didn't—because that's when my mother began to cry.

And cry.
And cry.
And cry.

That kind of scary sobbing is a combination of snort and whimper, which turns the nose red and bulbous and, in my mother's case, her blue eyes aquamarine against blotching skin. As a second grader, I see crying now and then on the playground, but it's really disconcerting to see a grownup crying. It was something I could not begin to understand when I saw it, or maybe ever.

What accounted for this almost allergic reaction?

You see, Mom remembered Donald E. from her childhood. He was "retarded" or MR. Sure, he was nice enough. She met him in elementary school, and he grew to be tall and kind of handsome. Brown hair and big brown eyes. And sweet, very sweet.

But Donald E. always had a bit of a blank stare. And he was rarely "in the group." I too have a blank stare now and then and am not always invited into the group. Sometimes it takes my teachers' prompting to get other kids to, say, play hopscotch or chase with me. They accuse me of throwing rocks and spitting. I counter that they call me different, and I don't like it.

Could it mean that I would be the next Donald E.? Mom said he walked across the stage at high school graduation, but she hadn't heard of him since. By any measure, he had essentially disappeared.

Poof!
Poof!
Poof!

When Mom heard these terms with respect to me, she cried because, way back then, in the 1970s to 1980s and until just recently, it was kind of a sentence. Not quite a death sentence but maybe like a prison sentence, a developmental limbo of neither heaven nor hell in which your prospects close in around you and your family like a six-by-six-foot cell. Put another way, it was purgatory for either the person who was labeled or his or her family.

People in your community looked at you, and their lips automatically pursed; and their heads moved slowly side to side in sympathy—no, pity.

Back then, in the old days, there were limits to what "retarded"—now ID—children were able, were expected, to do. The "retarded" kids would focus on crafts or learn "life skills." The teachers made sure they knew how to use tableware and clean their bottoms after using the potty. They had to be reminded to wash their hands.

If you ask me, those aren't quite life skills, but then no one has asked, and I am pretty good at one of the above, or maybe both. Every now and then, I must confess, I like to use my fingers to eat, but that's a kind of cultural thing you'll come to understand about me.

This way, different kids back in the day could grow tall, even handsome (Donald E. was square-jawed like a

Disney prince), but they were not in the group. They were pronounced permanent children. Come to think of it, that doesn't sound so bad to me, but it was something parents whispered about. Even the late President John F. Kennedy had a sister who kinda disappeared in this way, after a little surgery to keep her quiet.

Poor, poor Donald E., they'd say.

Poor boy.

Poor boy.

Poor boy.

Sometimes the other kids called people like Donald E.—and now me—retards. Ree-e-e-tards-s-s! If I tried to say it, it would come out "R-e-e-e-t-t-t-ards-s-s!" I also stutter, you see.

But the stutter (not too bad) was not why my mother was wailing, really, returning from the school that day, winding her six-year-old Honda Civic Hybrid up the road through hills and trees that suddenly seemed frightening, closing in on her. A Grimm's fairy tale without the fairies. If I were really MR, ID, or her own Donald E., would I be called mean names and fade away into the cloud puffs? Would I be limited, either by my own abilities, disabilities, or society?

Of course, I cannot articulate all this right now, but this is what was going on.

Mom called my father on the phone and cried all the way home from that hour-and-a-half-long meeting, not too long after an ARD, also known as a consultation to determine admission review and dismissal, which included a group of teachers and school officials. Come to think of it, it's no irony that if you add an *H* to the front, it spells *h-a-r-d* because my parents were about to find out about how hard this categorization process can be.

Oh, what was I saying?

These ARD meetings give people ants in their pants, my mother will later try to tell me. She would say parents who attend them tend to squirm because they feel very uncomfortable. Like Roz—the overbearing, snail-like character in *Monsters, Inc.*—school officials seem to be talking down to the families, saying they'll keep their watchful eyes on them, along with their children, really misfits.

I wasn't with Mom at the meeting because I was home sick that day with Daddy, but this is how it went: Dad kept telling Mom to calm down, calm down, calm down.

"It's going to be okay," he said, repeating when the cell phone reception failed a few times. "It's going to be okay. Just get home as soon as you can."

But was it going to be okay?

Meaning to be kind, the woman at school had printed out and given my mother some pieces of paper with community resources listed on them. She mentioned something called respite care so my mother and father could get help raising me, so grim was the prognosis.

So I could get help. Well, more specifically, so I could get on "the list" for services that would help in the "long term," the woman said. Now was the time to do this, she said sweetly, smiling gently—though almost robotic, as she clearly had said these same things to numerous parents before. No doubt, she too felt a burden. She had the test results, after all, and they did not look good.

Children such as me, she was saying, need support through adulthood and after their guardians died. Yeah, the lady was emphasizing my parents' own pending mortality, thank you very much. My future needed more thought today: simple job training, maybe a place to stay, hot meals, someone to give medicines on time—and to always make sure my bottom was clean.

You know, those are resources provided by private and public dollars—resources, at least early on, possibly paid for with insurance from my father's job or maybe with my mother's. I still don't know what he does at work, but he wears crisp shirts and shiny ties and sits in a cubicle. The people there are really nice and always say hi to me. Mom, on the other hand, dresses a bit like a flower child and teaches kids a lot older than I am. I understand she "goes teaching," as I always say. I get that.

Back at this meeting I was telling you about, when my mother reached for tissue to dab her moistening eyes, which by now were framed by a raccoon's mask of waterproof mascara, the woman trying to explain the situation had quickly pushed the entire box of tissues across the desks and said earnestly, "You're going to need them."

Mom was going to need them. She really would need a lot of tissues—that day and later. She needed them.

The lady was trying to be kind; but once again, it sounded very serious, very teachery, and all official. Mom would be crying some more beyond that drive home and more than once since she looked at me, very serious and teachery, and asked me, "Are *you* going to be okay?"

As if I totally knew.

At this point, I do not really know that I'm totally not okay. I just have a budding idea that okay is everyone's goal for most things around here.

Just so you'll know, Mom's rapid-fire succession of thoughts as she headed to meet my father, my sister, and me that afternoon were direct as rifle shots:

What if he can never financially support himself?

Who will feed him, making sure he drinks white milk for his bones and teeth, or get a Blue Bell ice-cream cup or canola-oil popcorn as a treat?

Will he have to live in a group home? Will they treat him gently? Will he cry for us when we're gone?

What if he can never sustain a relationship? No romance, no love? Can he ever be a parent? Will we ever be grandparents to his children?

So she was not crying because it is *bad* to be mentally retarded, MR, intellectually disabled, or ID. She was crying because she did not understand what it might mean for me and what she could do to help. Could I become a kind of Doogie Howser, MD, treating patients as a young savant, speaking as valedictorian at my high school graduation about my journey? This idea morphed into a wild scouring of her memory of high school graduation. Where was Donald E. that night? He did have on a maroon cap and gown, didn't he? He was so chill.

But what she began to see—because of that meeting, in an office with no windows and with paper reports in neat stacks on the desk—was well the opposite of the brilliant child-doctor or the happy Donald E.

Poof!
Poof!
Poof!

Suddenly she saw me again as the orphan I had been just a few years before, hovering in a corner, hands shaking in fear, crocodile tears welling in my eyelashes and falling downward, rivulets of warm salty water down a dirty face. She saw a deep, bleeding cut on the back of my head and freshly scalded skin on my left hand. She saw other marks, possibly from knives. And then the arm, the right one I favor when I walk or run, which she, on her darker days, suspects might be signs of an earlier wound. She imagines me being shoved or restrained and me screwing up my face in such pain and possibly screaming.

She did not know yet that it is I who will help her understand that it was not—and is not—bad as all that.

In fact, it is not that bad at all. It is, as "they" say, all good, really.

So I don't totally know, but I pretty much know some parts. This is my story.

Old Life, New Parents

My parents are *older* parents.

Dad is fifty-six; Mom is forty-nine. Anyone with an inkling of basic statistics and good, old-fashioned actuarial tables knows they likely will die sooner than I will. Really, everybody knows that. Together, struggling with the words, both of my parents kept wondering now who would take care of me then if I were, indeed, that person fixed forever in childhood?

A forever child left abandoned by what I had believed would be my "forever family," I landed with caretakers who really seemed to care. In fact, when I first came, they asked me what I wanted: food, toys, shoes. It was the first time anyone had asked me such questions, and it was way cool.

It was the first time someone was dabbing my nose, rapping about "soap and water," and, well, noticing me as something beyond a burden.

And I know by now that you're wondering too and asking if my parents should have known there might be trouble much earlier: was I a late-in-life baby, prone perhaps to disabilities, with afflictions missed or caused by amniocentesis? Did I suffer from fetal-alcohol syndrome, or was I a crack baby, as with many adoptions?

No. I don't think so, at least.

You see, I was adopted from China three and a half years ago, the second of two children my US parents adopted from Asia over a decade. Mommy says she couldn't have a baby in her tummy (she had e-e-endometriosis-s-s), so adoption was a way for her to become a mommy and for Daddy to become a daddy.

My parents had been waiting about three years for a second daughter, whom they would have called Grace for Mom's maternal and paternal grandmothers' middle names (and for the philosophical concept, which is nice if you think about it), but delays for any match at all continued.

One day, after feeling overwhelmed about the wait—"It was like our child [albeit still only theoretically] was being held hostage from us," Mom would later say—Mommy went to the waiting child list, agreed to a slightly older child than the first application stated, and completed an electronic wish list of sorts. The checks included possible disabilities, and she okayed cleft palates—which can be surgically repaired, along with any aftereffects supported in speech therapy—but not any more serious challenges such as muscular dystrophy or epilepsy. She feared her husband's and her work schedules and medical coverage might not cover extensive care.

Of course, she also would later admit she was not sure how to tend to a child with special needs, especially with old age not too far ahead. She just wanted their second child to get home. In what she later described as a leap of faith, she clicked "boy" as an option too. And yet she had already purchased a few knickknacks with the word *grace* on them and purchased her first child a James Avery charm with a little sister on it.

Within forty-eight hours came the adoption-agency call: "We think we have a child for you—and *it's a boy*!"

My mother, driving to a community college on the opposite side of town, had just hit downtown and could barely hold the cell phone while making a turn. She squealed with delight.

"He's very cute," the female voice on the other end of the phone said. "He's precious."

After that phone call, my mother called her husband. "Well…," she began.

Not long after, the adoption counselor e-mailed a photograph of a boy with a smile that left these strangers smitten. By that evening, after a hastily called meeting with my would-be dad and sister, I was *in*! Two months later, I was in the United States.

And it really made sense for them to go back to China, a place my would-be adoptive parents obviously knew, that big place halfway around the world from here that I see on a map of the world on my pillow.

For a really long time, China has had a one-child rule. The country is so busy providing housing, food, and jobs to so many people that the government suggested limiting families to one child each, which means that many girls (like my sister) and some boys (like me) were put into line to get new families from all over the world. Kinda like overstock goods in the sale bin. Then we would have housing, food, and places to work someday. More importantly, we would have someone to love and someone to love us.

The way the government of China keeps family sizes small is to have parents with more than one child pay a little more, like a tax. Paying more money discourages couples from making more babies, so the theory goes. As China's economy grows, some families have more children; but when my sister was born, and then when I was born, whoever's tummies we came from couldn't keep us. Or, in my case, maybe they thought something was wrong with me.

I don't know.

These American wannabe parents filled out all the paperwork as they had done once before, promising to take care of me, sort of like the "for better or worse" line when they got married back in 1988.

Then, as now, no one really understood how long forever can be, but it's a nice thought, and they certainly meant to honor it as they began to adopt a second "healthy" child.

Slow Takes a Long Time

I still remember the day I posed for the photographs my prospective adoptive parents would see. The grownups across the world told me that this would be for my new family, and I smiled and held up my right hand, forming a peace sign with two of my fingers. I was in front of a small yellow table, on a small chair, possibly to make me look bigger, and I was wearing a dark-blue plaid shirt and gray or tan corduroys. It's really hard to tell now, and that's the picture my parents used in the "East meets West" announcement they had a friend print up to mail to friends and family.

Next to me was a stuffed panda bear with a pink, or maybe faded red, bow.

I do not remember everything, but I do remember this. I was in a foster home at least once but would later suggest, as my communication abilities improved, that there were more. Like my sister, who was in a small orphanage, I had caretakers or nannies who made sure I ate and was protected from the elements, the cold or wet weather outside.

Now, they didn't always protect me from a smack, but I'll get to that in a moment.

I know, you're wondering, "What was wrong with you if you were a boy adopted in China to an American family? Isn't it true that boys were always preferred to girls over there?"

Good questions.

My parents were given very little information except that I was originally found in a market at a few months old and then, more recently under government care, that I pooped normally and was "curious" about—and "vied" for—things. The documents also said I was "sweet as pie." The Chinese authorities later said they could not tell me about any other caretakers or foster parents "for privacy reasons." Knowing my parents, they would have tried to send updates as I began to exhibit differences from my sister and to confirm I was loved. Only later will my parents realize that mysteries shrouding my early years included more than the number of caretakers.

Later, they did try e-mails; but about that time, the Chinese government (which was frustrated by citizens saying bad things about it) either did not allow them to go through to my last school, or the address changed. At least when my parents sent snail-mail letters and photographs of my sister to where she's from—Nanping Welfare Home in the Southeast, on the mainland across from Taiwan—they never came back, "return to sender." But the e-mails to the last place I attended, the semblance of a school, came back with gobbledygook. My parents do know that a box of clothing and toys had not made it by the time they arrived to collect my sister, so I guess you could say mail in any form can sometimes be unreliable in China. Knowing my parents as I do now, I know they wanted to let everybody know that I was all right, just as they had promised.

What more I am able to express about my past life right now is that I was abandoned, possibly more than once, but I do not know why and secretly wonder if I was bad. To this day, after all these years at this new place, I have a major fear of having it happen again; so I am always asking my parents when we are going to the store and if they take one different turn, "*Where* are we going?"

There is something else. I am always insistent: "Pl-e-e-e-ase *never* leave me!" My parents imagine that children who haven't experienced what I have would not be quite so concerned. I always punctuate my important, imploring comment with the question, "You are always coming back, right?" I even say this aloud when I am dropped off at school. The crosswalk attendants probably think I am nutty or that maybe my parents regularly leave me alone.

For their part, my ever-appropriate parents call me agenda-driven when they describe that characteristic to their friends. All I know is that I feel safer if I ask, and they try to tell me what's coming up next. A mini-sentry always on duty, ever mindful of exits, entrances, and paths, I mentally and continually cross-check what they say and what they do. So far, they always tell the truth.

At the same time, predictably, I still keep asking, "Where are we going?" "What are we doing?" "Then what?"

Oh yeah, I was also physically abused.

I have a scar on my left hand. From what I have been able to say, the woman I refer to as China Mom literally put my hand to the fire. I have a few other scars, a couple that look like inch-long cuts; but whenever my latest parents ask about those, I smile sheepishly and say, "I dunno." It seems I forget some things and am more willing to talk about others. Sometimes my parents think I'm afraid to say anything. They try to fill in the blanks but insist that they do not direct what I say. I offer details when I feel like it, at unexpected moments, most often at bedtime.

Maybe I am afraid of getting in trouble again, and I will give you one example as to possible reasons why.

China Mom once threw a green bowl at my head, and I have a deep scar in the upper left back part of my scalp as a reminder. I would say, if I knew such measurements, it is an eighth of an inch deep. I pointed it out to my new mom not long after I arrived. Up until that moment, it had been covered by my hair, and she gasped. We did not own any green bowls at my new house.

"Why did she throw the bowl at you?" American Mom asked—not that there is ever a valid reason to throw a bowl at your kid's head. Sure, as a parent, you might feel like it. You might even consider it. But you certainly don't do it. It is simply not the right thing to do. It is not in line with "time out" or "withdrawal of privileges" or anything from the book *How to Talk So Kids Will Listen & Listen So Kids Will Talk*.

No, sirree. No bowl-throwing there.

To explain the gash—which was healing but clearly a dent—I tried to tell Mommy that I might have done something wrong or made China Mom mad, probably because I kept wetting myself. But American Mom is not clear to this day if that was why, or if China Mom was frustrated by economic or emotional circumstances. China has had struggles in recent years, and who knows why she was assigned to me. Or maybe she was evil. So right after I told American Mom all this, she says, "If I saw that woman right now, I would say, 'Don't you *ever* hurt *my son* again!'"

I have her repeat that many times later that night and many evenings to come. We lie atop my bed in the dark and face the corner of the room and role-play, pointing our fingers toward this imaginary spot where China Mom—we imagine—is staring back at us defiantly, or perhaps hurtfully, insanely, or frightened.

She definitely wasn't qualified to take care of me.

All the same, we tell her off, getting more emphatic each time. Sometimes I'll direct my new mom's level of forcefulness. "Tell her again! Tell her again, 'Don't you ever hurt *my* son again!'" Sometimes I myself tell China Mom to stop, and then I seek reassurance from American Mom that I never have to endure that kind of meanness again.

"Son, we are forever. You do not have to worry," she will say.

I want the hall light left on because, as I explain, "I am scared of *goats*"—my word for ghostly things—and "I promise to always be a good boy." Being bad seems to make grownups mad. And when they get mad, I get sad.

I get scared too, out of my guts.

I do not know this even to this day, but my latest (and, I hope, last) mother waits to tell my latest (and, I hope, last) father about this exchange. She is shaken by the images I have put in her mind that night before we sleep: I, upstairs; she, down.

An analogy is slowly forming in her mind: the hieroglyphics of abuse. She, her husband, and their other child (the girl, who is going to be my forever sister) are thrust into the role of anthropologists, divining my past, one they hadn't imagined.

So by now, you know I was psychologically abused too.

Not long after I arrived in this country, my current and now *forever* parents took me to a homeopathic specialist, someone who tries to use nature's medicines—vitamins, herbs, oils—to heal. She put some drops on the inside of my lower arm and asked me to draw a picture. So I took the pencil and drew this room, rising up a few stories, showing where I was locked with a little baby. I call him Shah-rone and described him gurgling—"spitting," I always say. I described that we could not get out of the room. There was a rope involved, but I could not explain. And we saw China Mom walking away outside with some man. I do not know if he is her husband or an uncle, brother or older son, but I do sense that he is not my father.

I do not know, but it is this picture that leads to that before-bedtime conversation I just described.

What I do know is that they (the people in the picture and in my memory) walk far away, into the distance. And we watch them. I do not like China Mom; she terrifies me. But I sure do not want her to leave. What will happen to me if she doesn't come back? How will I get out of this room?

Later, I will try to describe to my mom about being tied up. I am trying to say that China Mom tried to keep me on that same green bowl, a pot maybe, so that I would not wet the blanket, and then on the floor where I slept, where I occasionally say I have a cover, a cloth maybe. At least that is what she thinks I am trying to say.

I bring it up one night. My new mom has come upstairs to tell me good-night, and I begin to tell her about this place where I and this other child, whom I often wonder about, were. I want to know if he will come with us someday to this new place where I am now lying side by side with this new caretaker, a woman I now usually call mommy. I wonder about Shah-rone; but first I have to wonder about where I will be tomorrow, next week, next month, and next year.

You see, I still pee a lot at night and wear Pull-Ups because of it. I have been peeing at night all my life from what I can recall.

When my American father and mother adopted me, I peed in the hotel bed right next to my American dad, where I was sleeping across from American Mom and the girl they said was my new sister.

They cleaned it up, pressing the white towels into the mattress repeatedly.

I peed the next night too. They cleaned it up again, this time putting dry towels underneath the fitted sheet.

I peed again.

The third time, the maids sort of smiled and shook their heads. I knew then, as I know now, that they did not think, *Poor child*. They thought, *Lucky child*, as all the people in China said to us as we prepared to go to my new home.

When the interpreter from the adoption agency asked me about the peeing, I nodded in recognition, shamefaced. The interpreter told them that I recognized I was doing it and did not want to. I still do not want to pee; I just do. My parents think maybe I sleep too soundly. Now I have plastic on my American bed, and sometimes I put on two Pull-Ups. I think I will stop peeing someday. Maybe I will just be able to hold it until the morning. But for now, I get up each morning, remove the Pull-Ups, and use wet wipes to clean my bottom. I bathe every night and like to be clean. No one has to teach me how good it feels to be clean versus dirty.

My first night in the hotel room with my new parents and the nine-year-old girl who was with them, I got a bath. The water was nice and warm and very sudsy. It turned brown from the grime that was on me. It would be several weeks before all the grime came off, and I grew to like baths, not just for the bubbles, but because I could play with my new, plastic toys.

I still play with my plastic toys every time I take a bath. Sometimes I look at the picture of that first bath, the bubbles, and my half-moon smile. I am smiling at the camera, and these new people—the man with brown hair, the woman with yellow hair, the little girl with black hair and black eyes like me—are laughing and calling me by my Chinese name, Guo, and another name they apparently like too.

It is a happy memory.

I like these people, I was thinking. *They know how to have fun.* That night, I got my first toothbrush.

When this yellow-haired woman with the pale skin put the brush to my teeth and gums, blood gushed out. You see, and I do tell her this later, I had never before brushed my teeth. And if you don't brush your teeth, it's a little bit like the scurvy described in books about pirates who haven't had oranges or Vitamin C—gums bleed, and teeth eventually pop out.

My gums bled for several days, but after gentler brushing, the bleeding stopped. With just a little attention, it seemed, the wounds healed. A few weeks later, my parents coaxed me into flossing my teeth, and soon enough, they went from yellow to white. As the months and then years passed, I would learn that these new people in this new country were obsessed with teeth. Once, when watching television, I said, "Listerine mouthwash," which is something I would get all my very own soon enough. This box, this television, spews out all kinds of products devoted to teeth. We have four TVs where we live. I do not distinguish between the shows and the commercials. I like to repeat dialogue from all of them.

If I were an anthropologist myself, I would write a report revealing that there is a tooth god these people are always trying to please. "These tooth tribes appear to believe that only white teeth can satisfy the all-powerful tooth god, whose only demand is the tribute of shiny porcelain teeth," I would write. With my twice-a-day brushings, my smile was just as big as the one that attracted them but just brighter. Soon the weak baby teeth—some protected by fillings or *seals*, as this teeth-worshiping tribe called them—would begin falling out, only to be replaced by strong new ones I hope to keep.

Yes, I like these people, silly as some of their rituals are. Have I told you about handwashing? OMG, I am always being told to wash my hands "with soap and water." They call what I logically call *han-a-tizer* hand sanitizer.

Don't get me started about handwashing and wet wipes in the car. Suffice it to say that I accommodate them in their germ-fighting ceremonies too because they usually accommodate me.

Old House, New Life

Let me tell you about my house now.

About twenty years-old, it has more than one floor, like the picture in the house I drew. But there are many differences. My bedroom—my very own and my first—is on the second floor on the west side of the house, near a major Texas city. The sun goes down every day outside my very own window. I have bright-yellow walls and navy-blue curtains, striped dust ruffles in primary colors, hardwood floors, and dark wood furniture. The bed is very tall, and someday American Mom will tell me that she found the frame in an antique store and that Dad had slats specially made and measured for a new mattress. Once owned by people who typically were not as tall as people today, it has never been without plastic on the mattress, even before my inaugural pee in it, so it really is a "brand-new" pad. These people are not rich, and our house is small, about 1,800 square feet, but so much bigger than any place I ever lived. Middle class to me is upper class to the me of the old days.

We have a kitchen, two bathrooms, two other bedrooms, a small dining room, and a living area.

But back to the most important element. My room is nice on the inside, but it also is nice on the outside. It has pretty views. Sometimes I sneak up from bed and watch my mother come home at night from teaching, which she does for boys and girls who have already graduated high school. Somehow I know that she can see the outline of my shadow watching her, and she imagines me smiling at her arrival. I know I am supposed to be in bed asleep, filling my bladder for its next release, but I am happy looking out from my room. She is walking in the right direction, unlike the woman in my pencil drawing for the homeopathic specialist.

In the front of my house, there is a view of a hill above a creek. There are always birds outside, as well as squirrels, deer, and wild hogs. Last spring, some cardinals built a nest outside our dining-room window. The nest had three small eggs, which turned into three small birds. Both the daddy bird and mommy bird would take turns feeding them. We watched the family for weeks, and I drew a picture of their "house." I kept asking questions about what they were doing, and then the day they all left, I really wanted to know where they went.

"They went to a new larger nest," my parents assured me. "They are growing up, just like you."

I like the sound of the word *forever* in English too. I do not know yet if or when I will live somewhere else, but mainly I know—have to know and need to know—that this is where I belong, that I will not be flying to another place. These nice people and this nice little girl, who is getting taller herself, will keep reassuring me of that. Sometimes I think they read my mind.

I have a lot of toys. Many Legos, an Erector set, and books. I have dozens of books, mostly hand-me-downs, including a few Dr. Seuss books in Mandarin and English. *Green Eggs and Ham* is just as funny in either language. I like how the main character keeps saying he will not try green eggs and ham. And when he does, he likes them! He says, "No! No! No!" And then next he says, "Yes! Yes! Yes!" That is *so* funny.

I like to observe when things are funny; or if I hear people laughing, I will laugh along, not always knowing why but doing it all the same.

Ha-ha-ha. It's like a drumbeat.

Sometimes, when I laugh, I sort of cough out the sounds, making what you might call a guffaw. Laughter is a good thing.

At the same time, some of my teachers say I am ID, retarded, because I do not "recognize plot" in a story. Oh, they do not put it quite that way because I have no idea what *plot* means. I can tell you what happens in a story, but if you ask me to tell you the plot, I will give you that blinky look and put my lips together. Still, they say that my academic performance and language skills mean that I need special education. I could not pass a Texas standardized exam (it is called the STAAR). If you threatened to starve me or bang my head or send me away, all things I understand very clearly, I could not do it.

I could tell you about *Green Eggs and Ham* and the other Seuss books. I love to read *The Cat in the Hat* too. Reading that book, I have asked many times, "Where is the mommy going?" My American mother used to wonder that too when she read the very same book as a child on a German military base in the late 1960s. She might someday share that she too worried about her emotionally absent parents—that it is normal to want to know where they are, even if they are not always nice. All I need to know in this very moment is that we are reading together and relating across the expanses of geography, both emotional and physical.

Deep down, when I cling to her for assurance, she is holding me for the same thing. Across the decades, turning pages of time, she is reassuring the lost little girl she sometimes felt like with the hugs for which she always longed. I might never know that is part of her motivation for reaching out to me from the beginning. For now, she simply says that the *Cat in the Hat* Mommy had to go to work and that the babysitter is in the other room for just a moment and that Mommy is "always coming back."

Always coming back. I like the sound of that phrase too. I say it a lot. I say things a lot in triplicate, in threes, in a rhythm, a kind of musical way to reassure myself.

Not long after the day of the ID report, about which I know nothing, I would be talking about my childhood again, going back to those days when Mommy asks gingerly, "Will you ever tell me more about your time in China before you came to your forever house?"

And as there is an official report saying that one of my target educational goals is to "identify plot," I reply, "We-el-l-l, my story has many *elements.*" Then I add, "Maybe someday."

My mother remains silent, thinking, *I have to tell your father and sister what you just said! There is so much more to this child than any of us adults can see.* She knows that. I do not quite know that, although she thinks I know a lot more than any tests can capture.

Even my sister, twelve years old at the time, in a whispered conversation I do not hear (nor would understand), tells my parents after the day when the "mentally retarded" phrasing is used, "He is *not* retarded. He is just catching up is all." Then she continues to ponder what I have taught her, if anything. It was she, after all, who insisted on a second child, a sibling, a boy or a girl.

A few days later, my sister adds, "Just think, if we didn't have him, I wouldn't have learned not to be jealous or how to share."

Of course, I know that in my own way. Sure, life so far has naturally taught me to be cautious, but other than that, I'm thinking things are going awfully well.

A List of My Favorite Things

So as of this month, I am now a special-ed kid.

I do not really know that term yet; I just know that I leave class a lot.

A few days after I came to America, my independent school district required a test to put me into school—English as a second language programming, as they called it. I am blessedly oblivious to the gauntlet of acronyms and euphemisms through which my parents are beginning to enter.

The nice lady—neat hair, glasses, and a smile—said to me, in English, something along the lines of, "Tell me what is happening in this picture." I guess you could say she was asking me about the plot. It was a picture of a house with some stairs. There were some things going on in it. Motion, I recall. Maybe a young child moving. A bicycle.

I had proudly just written a few Chinese symbols with marker on a board in the waiting area, but now, facing the picture, I just stared. I didn't say a word in any language. I guess I thought, *Can't she see what is happening in this picture? She is the nice lady with neat hair, glasses, and a smile. Why is she asking* me*?*

Adults!

I spoke Mandarin fluently. My mom's Chinese friend said I sounded older, more mature, than the age the Chinese even said I was when I came, which would have been seven. But when I stared at the picture, not knowing much in English by this time, I was silent, finally looking at the woman, my mother, and my sister then back.

They think I do not know what is going on because I am seemingly noncompliant; I am thinking. They think I do not want to play along, but I am thinking, *Why don't they want to play along?*

I don't want to be rude or anything after all. That does not go over well with grownups. But are they stupid or what? *Look at the picture! It's obvious what is happening!* I am thinking.

Later, my new mother will say to my father, "Some days it just seems like he's waiting for us to get it!"

I would have to agree, now that I have more perspective. These big people just don't always know what *it* is. But I really am a patient person. I have learned to wait—and dream—because I have not had a choice.

Let me share a funny story my parents now repeat to people.

Once, they heard a *boom* sound upstairs. My father asked, "What *was* that sound?" He wanted to know what

Slow Takes a Long Time

had happened, and if I was okay. Instead of telling him what had fallen (a big book), I replied in a literal way, as I often do, "Boom!" I said.

I still do not know why they think this is so funny, so I just will repeat in triplicate, as I often do:

"Boom!"

"Boom!"

"Boom!"

There is another moment my parents still laugh about, not in a mean way. Daddy was trying to teach me baseball in the front yard. He had purchased plastic bases from Academy and was pitching to me across home plate. Of course, I had never played baseball, nor had I watched a game on television or attended a game yet.

He made the pitch. The bat connected with the ball. No, the crowd didn't roar, but dad went, "Go home! Go home!"

I set the bat down and walked to the porch and went inside.

Well, he said, "Go home," and I did. I still am not sure why he changed his mind and pointed to where I was standing and said, "This is home."

I often have different interpretations, but in this case, I know where home is.

I love to sing, and I inherited my sister's first iPod, which is hot pink. I especially like the song "Shake Your Boom Boom." I am partial to consonants.

"Mom, what's 'shake your boom boom' mean?"

I knew two English words when my American parents got me: *mama* and *bridge*. I knew *mama* because, as I said, I remember having at least one of those, maybe a foster mom, I am not sure. She was the lady who was mean to me, the one I called China Mom. American Mom says *mama* is an international word; I couldn't care less about the origins of the word. I am just glad to have one of my own.

I cannot tell you why I knew the word *bridge*; but for the first few days I was with my would-be American parents, I would see bridges as we drove around in Central China, near my home city of Luoyang, in Henan Province, about two hours' plane ride from Beijing. The city is a mix of squalor, shanty houses, lovely parks, and modern administrative buildings—many seemingly from the Communist revolution under Mao.

Everyone knows Mao.

There are cars and bikes everywhere.

"Bridge!" I would yell excitedly.

Yeah, I like to build things, and I like to point out bridges. I am excited when I see bridges. I smile the smile they saw in the stamp-sized photo of me when they were contacted by the agency. It is a smile that envelops my face and nearly closes my already small eyes as it spans my face and seems to streeetch to both ears.

The third word I began to say well was *baba*, or "daddy" in Mandarin. I liked my new daddy. He held me and comforted me, so much so that when he left the hotel with my sister, leaving me with my new yellow-haired Mom, I screamed. I raged. I would not stop. *Don't take this nice man from me. He is so nice. He is tall and smells like soap and has a nice smile.* Well, that was what I was thinking.

I went on like that for thirty minutes. A piercing scream—bloodcurdling, as they say in horror books. I would not stop screaming. If anyone could hear me, they needed to come to the rescue and reunite me with that nice man.

Finally, with this other woman, the one I will think of as American mom, in tears, she scooped up all thirty-seven pounds of me and took me down to the pool, where the new baba was. Already in the swimsuit they brought with them—made in China—I plunged in the smaller pool and grabbed the multicolored plastic inner tube. I was now happy. The distress call and subsequent rescue were a complete success. There were fake plastic palm trees near the pool with fake plastic bananas. I wanted to eat them but did not understand why I could not. Recently, cuddling with American Mom before bed, I asked her why.

"Plastic doesn't taste good," she explained.

"Why were they plastic?" I asked back.

Good question. As always, the conversation flitted somewhere else after that.

But my happiness in the pool back with American Baba, the first non-uncle I recall, was real. He has such kind green eyes. He's the one I slept (and peed) next to those first few nights. He snored very loudly, like a bear, which would later make me think of Mr. Berenstain Bear. He helped give me my first real bath. And I slept and dreamed next to him, where it felt safe, soothed by the rhythm of his deep, contented breathing.

And I peed again.

By the third day, these Americans took me to a Chinese store in search of Pull-Ups. They looked everywhere. Apparently, Pull-Ups were not as popular in China as they were in America. We saw toddlers peeing and pooping in cigarette-ash cans outside the store. I even squatted and peed on a crowded street my first day. I had to go, so naturally, I pulled down my shorts, baring my behind and squatting like a girl. We have a picture of that moment, however brief, too. Well, I had to go. And nobody saw or said anything, so it was okay.

Ahhh, perfect relief.

From then on, however, these new people wanted to capture my nighttime pee in these fresh white cushions. And they found some: Chinese Pull-Ups to last us the rest of the two weeks we stayed there. There was—and is—something comforting about them, swaddling clothes for the precious baby. For most of the time, I was a koala clinging to Baba's mobile, treelike six-foot-one-inch frame.

When I met my new parents, I had on a dingy T-shirt and worn cotton shorts and girls' sandals. They had purchased some clothes from America—again made in China—but the suitcase went missing for what turned out to be a week, so we had to go to a Chinese store for new clothes and underwear. You see, I didn't wear underwear. My mother will tell me much later that underwear is a relatively new fashion invention: guys wore breeches for the longest time; and women, later, pantaloons well into the 1800s. Sure, it had been invented by my adoption in summer 2008 but not necessarily affordable by a poor kid with limited resources.

I had to get used to underwear by day and the Pull-Ups at night.

Not only did I feel cleaner, I felt adored. This new set of people was paying so much attention to me. I liked that feeling. Top to bottom, this civilization tended to its people.

The Beijing-based Chinese-English interpreter from the adoption agency and the driver helped select the new clothes, including a pair of blue plastic shoes with daisy imprints on them, sort of like Crocs (yes, all labeled "Made in China"). The new parents wanted to redirect me from what I someday would learn as the "flowers are for girls" theme. But once I saw those shoes, I was in love, and there was no turning back.

Later, after we got to Texas, where I now live, I told the neighborhood Chinese restaurant owner—in Mandarin—that I liked my new parents. "Why?" she asked? I said, "Because they got me two new pairs of shoes." Yeah, being American, they quickly added a pair of Velcro athletic shoes with socks when we got home.

Two pairs of shoes—now *that* is living!

Special Education

I have been through many pairs of shoes. I am a high-energy boy and have picked out Green Lantern and Spiderman shoes, Nike, and Sketchers. Honestly, I don't know about the brand; I just got those because of the colors and because some of them lit up. Plus, they were easy to put on and take off. For my second-grade class picture, my mother picked out some blue velvety Shaun White shoes from Target with shoelaces. One more failing the school psychologist pointed out in that fateful meeting with Mom was that I was always walking down the halls with my laces untied. Maybe a respite-care worker would have to keep them tied.

A friend of my parents would scoff at that, saying, "They all walk around with untied shoes."

Another said, "My son is in his twenties, and he still walks around that way!"

I guess they are "retarded" too.

Another reason for the diagnosis of developmental or emotional challenges is that I drew a picture of a knife. The lady at the school who said that I was ID gently nudged the picture forward to my mom to show her, as if it were exhibit A of my disability, as if she were expecting a reaction of horror.

"Oh, that's from the television series *Man vs. Wild*." My mom lightly explained my admiration of how the show's star, Bear Grylls, could fashion all sorts of implements to survive in the wild. She remembered too that a portrait of me at Legoland near San Diego included a gigantic sword—my choice. I seem to like such weapons, a possibly dangerous inclination beyond the average boy.

The school official/criminal profiler slowly and stiffly pulled back the drawing, as if returning exhibit A to the future-serial-killer-evidence files labeled, "Liked Knives at an Early Age." Still, the verdict for now, at least, is split.

Oh, Dad made me a mixtape CD of my favorite songs to go along with the Chinese folk songs. Bruce Springsteen's "Growing Up" is one of my favorites, but I say it as "groaning up." He and Mom love how earnestly I belt out the words, pitch-perfect, they say. I also like the Beatles' "Hey Jude" and "Yellow Submarine" and "Here Comes the Sun."

My father has long asked, "Shouldn't he have a Chinese tutor along the way? Could it just be a language barrier at this stage?" By year's end, there would be check marks in every category in which I lag: in reading, writing, and mathematics. I would be "placed" in third grade.

No, they say. They know how to teach, and I am struggling.

If you are not convinced as to my "retardation," there are other reasons it was highly suspected. When one of the ladies discussing my needs asked me how old I am, I said, "Sixty!" I stretched up my head, pulling it like a string out of my spine to show her how tall I was—progress.

Later, my mother told her that was how much I weighed then. But the lady repeated the story to the group at another trial—oops, ARD meeting.

Oh is that "hard"?

In conclusion, ladies and gentlemen of the jury, I do not tie shoes well, and I use fuzzy math for my age in lieu of tree rings or carbon dating.

You see, my parents never have stressed my age, thinking the Chinese documents might have been wrong. On good days, they want to believe a guardian angel forged or switched my documents to spirit me out of danger. On good days, they make me a modern-day Moses. Instead of a basket, I was smuggled out of danger in a Boeing jet.

I repeated first grade. They did not want me to feel self-conscious, so they stressed my grade and my weight. Finally, after I said I was "sixty," an adolescent psychiatrist told my parents we could pick an age appropriate to my grade and developmental peer group, so I am now turning eight.

"Happy birthday!" they said when we celebrated at Chuck E. Cheese's.

When they asked, "How old are you now?" I replied, "Eight!" proudly, not skipping a beat.

Now that my birthday is so close, I ask for an Xbox, but my parents say that is expensive, so I will have to ask Santa Claus. That sounds practical. He, Santa, is very practical too, however. He has given me clothes and socks from Old Navy. I like clothes to this day, but I also like to think about electronics. All of my age-appropriate peers talk about the toys they have. And my sister has a Wii and lets me race. I love my sister; she is the best sister ever. She is my favorite, maybe because she looks more like I do; and sometimes, when she is not mad, she says I am cute.

Oh, I digress.

Not really.

To me, it is not digressing; it's just following my brain. But the ominous report stands. Unbeknownst to me, it sounds pretty hopeless, frankly, which is why my parents are so worried.

Let's move back to more cheerful topics connected to this new family: my sister.

As mentioned, she is from China too, but she came when she was a baby, ten months old, in February 2000. After repeating second grade to compensate for malnourishment-related delays, she is now in sixth grade and earns mostly As. She is very pretty. We have the same color of hair and eyes, but hers are rounder and mine smaller. Sometimes she rolls her eyes and uses "a tone," as my parents call it, and tells me no. Someday my mother might tell me about how my sister initially wanted them to leave me in China after the trial run. She simply did not like it that I appeared to want to stay permanently. She was jealous and angry, even though she had thought she wanted a baby sister or brother.

She bosses me and tells me to "be quiet!" But that does not bother me because I know, deep down, she loves me because once in the pool, when my head went under, she grabbed and protected me. My parents say she actually gets credit for saving my life even earlier because they were not going to adopt a second child, and my sister kept begging them to do so and then agree to me when they saw that picture of me—one big smile. I do not believe that I will see my sister in any other way than I do now. She is the nicest and best sister ever. And I love her very much. Of all the people I know how to hug today, I hold on to her the very longest until she squirms to wrest herself way, laughing.

I understand sisters. My documents claim I was in a program to learn to bond with younger children as preparation for a blended family. I often ask American Mom about when she was a little girl, although I call it "when you were a little sister." And she will tell me what she did, like playing kickball or acting out scenes from movies, mostly musicals such as *The Sound of Music* and *West Side Story*. She also told me that most of her family is "all gone" now, which is why our foursome is so precious to her. As I explain it, three of them "got died."

I ask similar questions to American Dad. "When you were a little boy, did your daddy take you camping too?"

I have a miniature green John Deere truck, which I drive around in circles. "Daddy, when you were little, did Santa bring you a car too?"

"No, son. I didn't have a car until I was eighteen," Daddy replies, growing thoughtful. "It was white too, a 1968 Ford Thunderbird. I worked after school to pay for gas and insurance."

Whatever that is, parents always are adding details I deem unnecessary.

I love movies such as *The Karate Kid* and always ask my parents about different parts, assuming they know all the answers about character motivation, appearing to believe the actors, in some ways, are all real life. I relate to them sometimes. I do not differentiate between television shows and commercials, sometimes seamlessly saying—in a high, radio-announcer voice—"We'll be right back" then repeating, "We'll be right back."

Back to real life, I love all my teachers. True, some people on my ARD team obsess about untied shoes or that I cannot remember my parents' phone numbers and my propensity toward collecting knives. I do not, and might never, know the concern swirling around me, the multiple meetings, the thick documents warranting worrying words of what-ifs. Other than making sure I never leave this place—this clean place of plenty of food, comfortable shoes, smiles, soapy smells, soft beds, and toys—I have no concerns at all.

Okay, maybe the overarching concern is pretty big: I never want to leave here. I always watch for my parents' cars as the bus drives up. They have taught me how to walk home and put a key in my backpack in case they are ever late, but mostly, they are early. Mom will tell Daddy and Sister, "I remember being the last one waiting for a ride after band practice, so I don't want you all to experience that."

I am proud that I can give any substitute bus driver directions. Unlike Hansel or Gretel, I do not need bread crumbs; I have an exacting visual memory to guide me home, like a skylight in the dark. I am always scanning my environment, making sure nothing bad will ever happen again. I look at the horizon, the scenery, and I look at faces. Therein lies all the information I will ever need.

I do not usually use these words. In fact, I do not use most of the words in this story, but I feel like I am living life's lottery. When I play Wii, no matter what my score, I shout, "I win! I win! I win!"

I always feel like a winner.

So while I was able to love people before (I suspect all children do), I was not able to love them as long as I wanted to. As hard as I tried, they kept leaving. As hard as they were toward me, I wished that they wouldn't go. Even when I kept my eyes on them, they seemed to vanish, never to be seen again. I really loved them. And now I love these new people, these Americans, and I have for a long time, now three and a half years, which feels like forever.

Forever, in my way of looking at things, is a really, really long time. And it is beautiful.

In America Now

Sometimes I actually say, "I am in America now." No, I don't mean it in a geopolitical way. I am not jingoistic or anything like that. American exceptionalism is too complex a topic for most of us anyway, something better left for the late teens or talk radio. I do not even know what that is. Or, at least, my geopolitical way is that I am glad I am here, and I have told my family that I do not want to go back. I do not have anything against China per se; I just did not have the best time while I was there, and maybe some American kids have had similar experiences here.

I remember saying good-bye to my last class, a cluster of boys and girls, some with curved spines and shaved heads with fresh surgical stitches, all very kind. They gathered around me, like they do with the winner at *American Idol*'s season's end, knowing it would be my last day; and they were wishing me luck, each seemingly invested in one another's future rescue. First, I was lucky to be picked. Then I was lucky that my prospective family became my adoptive family and came to get me.

I remember that day clearly. I was wearing a white T-shirt and jeans bought at Dollar General weeks before. Cuffed at the ankle, the jeans gave me a kind of James Dean look just above my feet, now covered by my floral Croc knockoffs. I was carrying a Mickey Mouse backpack with larger Lego knockoffs and let my admirers pass the items around, never taking my eyes off my new possessions. They took and cupped the brightly colored plastic shapes in their hands, as if seeing gems for the first time.

My father filmed this scene on his video camera. Somewhat solemnly, I made a brief speech in my regionally tinged accent. Later, the interpreter would translate that I had told the other children "not to cry for me," that it was going to be okay.

And it has been. I walked out of that institution with my chest out, head held high. I was *chosen*, and I knew it then as I know it now, retarded or not. ID or not. This, I know.

I still talk about "when you came to get me in China" or "when I came to you in China."

For one thing, *my* new world is very stimulating. I love *SpongeBob* and *Man vs. Wild* and *Spy Kids* on DVD. I am in Cub Scouts and have made a small survival campground in our tiny backyard and what Dad calls my Stonehenge in the front, with rocks positioned in purposely mysterious patterns. I have made spigots for an imaginary campfire from sticks, connected low-hanging branches with dog leashes, and I have a green plastic plate and cup from the

Scouts store and a white fork and knife. With Mother Nature's architecture and campsite, I am expanding my safe space, the spaces here more welcoming than the tighter ones I once knew. Those images still come to me in my dreams or in a moment when I lose sight of the familiar.

I have a very nice bus driver too. I have had two others at least, but this lady always is on time and greets me. "Good morning!" she says. She lets me tell her what is on my mind—mostly SpongeBob—or that my mom will pick me up later. Twice I have told her I am walking home. I have a house key in my backpack. When I have walked home (we practiced first), I ran. Just to play it safe, I weave and bob into the wild bamboo lining our streets like a Marine in a firefight, camouflaging myself to become a more difficult target for the enemy who lurks. Since I take such precautions, I do not know why the neighbors' dogs bark so much. I asked my mom, and she said, "They are saying hello."

"They are saying hello, Ma?" I ask for reassurance.

"They are saying hello," she replies, sometimes feeling like the narrator in the PBS TV series *Caillou*. It isn't always easy for grownups to explain either, but I do not really understand that yet.

In my house, we repeat questions and answers all the time, at least three times but sometimes more. There is a cadence to my asking and my family's answering, akin to a theme song that is now our quartet's reassuring anthem.

When the teachers told my parents I was ID and my parents said that maybe I was just tired because the school I go to required a 6 a.m. pickup, they offered to have me go on the "short bus." It would not have saved much time off my schedule, but my parents—still unbeknownst to me—opted to begin driving me to school. It would give me forty-five more minutes of sleep, and I would not have to have a new bus driver. "He has had so much change," they reasoned. Within days, I begin arriving at school as if I were a rock star emerging from a stretch limo. I greet all the crossing guards and wave back to whomever parent is doffing his or her cap.

"I love you, Daddy."

"I love you, Mommy."

When Sister comes along on the way to her school, I tell her "I love you" too. She sinks into the seat, smiling.

I like the animals I see from the bus and car and the ones closer to home. The first night I was here, I met two cats inside the house. I lifted the young one up by the tail. I do not know this yet, but my mother was watching how I was with animals. Murderers, she keeps telling my father, all hurt animals in their early years. So she was watching me, shuddering at the thought of a *Dateline NBC* interviewer asking, "What was he like as a little boy? Did he pull cats' tails?" I did do not know this. I saw the tail, grabbed it, and the cat went aloft. This is on my dad's film from those first days. Sadly, that very same cat, Millie—or Milagro (for *miracle* since she was rescued at three weeks and bottle-fed for a few more)—died at age fifteen. Her successor, Edith, is now my favorite. A calico, she purrs and reaches for me when I get home. "She likes you," Mom says, still eyeing me warily, watching for the telltale *sign*. I kind of pull on Edith or do not always use a "soft" touch when I pet her, but she keeps approaching me, rolls on her back, paws forward, beckoning me to pet her. I try to be gentle then say, "Look, Ma! Edith likes me!" Then I follow up with, "Why does she like me?"

Meaning of Life

I ask a lot of questions, including meaning-of-life queries.

As with the late Millie the cat, death has been part of my life in America, but I seem to handle it okay. I had a grandmother and aunt who left my life—the first to cancer, and the second to depression—although I only know that they died because they were "sick." Rupert, our big, fat black-and-white dog, died after Millie, and then Shadow, another dog who showed up here before I did. I do not know that part of his story yet, but he came up, as country dogs do, all matted and flea- and tick-infested with a broken chain tied around his neck, like a chain-gang escape. He cowered when my father spotted him but later became my companion that first year. That's what I know: "Shadow died. He was my friend. He would go walking with me." But I seem Zen about it all, my parents will tell me later. They think I have a feeling about the afterlife or a sense that the two are barely separate spheres.

Buddha was a part of my life in China. I know how to press the insides of my hands together, touching the tips of my fingers to my chin and bow. I have a jade Buddha necklace just like my sister's on the typical silky red string ubiquitous in Asia. I know about Jesus—well, that's he's "like Buddha," or maybe the latter studied the former's teachings about living in the moment while staying connected to God. My parents drag me to a temple where they're always talking about Jesus and somebody named Luther. I like going to the front to get blessed. My parents won't let me drink the wine.

I do not know this yet, but Mom is on the fence about "organized" religion, the part where God has lesser say than the humans. She grew up in "church" and yammers on about hypocrisy she's encountered along the way. She does, however, cling to the spirituality, God, and prayer. Some days, she tiptoes us into the nearby Catholic Church, dips her fingers in the holy water, as we do too, and lets us buy candles for a quarter to light. She'll write a note listing pains or prayers to whomever reads those. Of course, I cannot know this yet; but so often, my name, my sister's, and Dad's are on those papers, as were my late grandmother's and aunt's.

She wants me "healed," whatever that means, and just really doesn't know that I am healing her.

Oh, at this church, next to the wall up front, there's a statue of a man with a crown of thorns and some bleeding gashes of his own, like mine, and then one with a woman in a blue robe. The air-conditioning unit in this chapel is loud and scares me a little, but I always want to go back. The kneelers make lots of noise hitting the floor, and I have always liked noise—except for bathroom hand dryers or institutional air-conditioners, which seem to stir a bad memory or, at the very least, hurt my ears. You could say I like the noise I get to make versus the noise I cannot control. New Mom is similarly sensitive to loud noise, especially loud voices, the tones of yelling. In that, she says, we are absolutely related.

Dad likes the ritual and the sermons of Lutheran Sunday services, so he follows along with the paper program and sings the songs, even when the music isn't turned on where we sit, at a distance in the foyer, in case I want to talk. We have a nice swing set outside this place of Buddha and Jesus and nice people; and my sister—iPod in her ear—will walk me out there if I cannot be still in the foyer, where I am told to whisper. The swings squeak in a soothing way, like a hawk calling its mate. Or maybe the call comes from parents beckoning a beloved child, their voices echoing against the portable buildings planted nearby.

One Sunday morning, we sat in the balcony. When it was time for the offering, for us to put the check or cash in the envelope and pass it around, there was no usher. So I took the plate and walked it downstairs to the front. They figured I would have handed it to an usher, but I decided to deliver it directly.

My parents were sitting upstairs and had not noticed my extended journey until the pastor had begun to speak, and I deliberately walked up front and handed him the plate. My mother's cheeks burned red. My father uttered, "Oh no!" But the congregation chuckled, and a lady sitting nearby said, "How cute!"

The school psychologist, coincidentally a church member, was near the front too. She looked up to the balcony and smiled.

"Look!" I yelled. "I know *her*!"

Thanks to my survival instincts and self-sufficiency, I know when to step up and get the job done.

Even if I am retarded, I have a few ideas for doctoral dissertations in my mind. They might help people who find loud noises frightful. One day, after the school's assessment of my disability, I very ably regaled my sister, father, and mother about public restrooms with hand dryers versus paper towels.

I was so earnest and detailed in my presentation. They were nodding, most impressed. Then they began laughing, certainly not insensitively because of my quasi phobia about loud hand dryers but because of how reasonably I made the case for thinking ahead before using the restroom in certain public places. I, the kid who had been proclaimed as special-needs, was receiving their full and special attention. I clearly had given it much thought and most sincerely wanted to make the case in order to be of assistance.

Slow Takes a Long Time

This child, suddenly a young man, was proudly presenting years of research on something that meant a great deal to him, they thought. My version of my life's work: "A Meditation on Companies Which Have Invested in Noisy High Technology." They remembered my first days in the public school, calling and crying from school after the large blowers in the school gym had set me off. They knew I did not like loud, sudden noises. At the same time, they knew I made a lot of noise, a seeming contradiction. But here I was, ticking off the names of major stores, restaurants, and even theme parks in my very large state with the loudest dryers. Then I figured out that wiping one's wet hands on one's clothes would do just as well.

- Target
- Office Depot
- Some parts of SeaWorld of Texas
- The Cheesecake Factory
- CVS Pharmacy
- The Palladium movie theater in San Antonio
- Dairy Queen
- Macy's

"I don't have to go to the bathroom in those places," I explained. "You don't like those sounds either, do you?"

"No, we don't," my parents said. "Good job, son."

This is only based upon current research. I am an ongoing student of hand dryers in public restrooms. We do not have those at our house.

When I know we might encounter some, I make sure to relieve my bladder or bowels before I know we are going to those places. If we go to a new place, I ask my parents if they know about the hand-drying accommodations.

This is market research by a little market researcher, a specialist in the field of survival. Dozens of times, I recount the list of places with loud electronic hand dryers in them. I have asked family friends how they view these machines. Forewarned, they smile. "No, we don't like them either," they might say.

Later, the night of a day spent at SeaWorld, with and without these hand dryers, a memory came to my mother. She was four years old. The family was stationed in Frankfurt, Germany, in a three-bedroom apartment at an army post. Her father had driven to work, and her two sisters had already walked to school, and it was a still morning. Before returning to bed, her mother had flushed the toilet. It kept running and running, the sound of the water a constant, endless swoosh. To her, it could have been ghosts winding their way down the hall to her bed. She curled her toes to secure the sheets at the bottom of the bed and began crying.

Her mother told her from the other room, "Be quiet. I'm trying to sleep."

Mommy began to cry, with the crying becoming louder as the toilet monsters continued to hum hauntingly, seeming to get nearer.

Finally it happened.

Her mother appeared above the bed and popped her on her bare behind with the bristles of a brush, the act of a parent craving sleep in an era in which such punishment was equal to the crime of interruption.

"Be quiet, or I'll give you something to cry about."

Whimpering softly, Mom, the young girl, pulled the covers over her head. The toilet eventually stopped its eerie sound, the goats or ghosts temporarily silenced either by the sheets, sleep, or all the years since.

Based upon my age alone, whatever it is, I might be a bachelor, but I have a bachelorette. Her name is Giselle. She is the girl I have loved in second-grade class. Brown hair and brown eyes to match. In pencil, I have written her name in letters about three-inches high on my bedroom wall—twice. It seemed the natural thing to do. I dream about her a lot. She isn't my first "girlfriend"; the other was a seventeen-year-old barista at Starbucks. She had curly blonde hair and pretty blue-green eyes. I told Mom I wanted to take her to dinner and a movie and give her a penny.

But now I want to take Giselle to dinner and a movie, and Mom finally told the older girl, with me in the car, at the drive-through that "it" was "over." She smiled and said,

"You don't love me anymore?" And I smiled, so it was all very friendly. When we go through the drive-through, I order a kid's hot chocolate, "not too hot." Sometimes I play hide-and-seek with my ex-girlfriend, burrowing my face beneath my hoodie or backpack. We remain friends. I hope she still has the coin.

Giselle is the one for me—although I don't know my mother now fears I might not marry because I am, well, "retarded," and might be in a special home, practicing life skills, doing crafts, and being in that group for the rest of my life. All that instead of being a dad. I ask my mom if Giselle can come live with us in my room. She says yes. I ask my mom if I can kiss Giselle. She says no.

Apparently, you have to be married to do that. Later, however, I tell her that Giselle and I exchanged "I love yous."

She smiles, and I smile, Dalai Lama–like, my dimples coming to life again.

One day, in fall 2011, some boys in my class were calling me "different." I did not know what that meant, but I did not like their tone or their faces. I wanted to respond in full measure, so I picked up a rock and threw it at them. I also said a bad word, something I had heard in a movie the weekend before. My parents had not known I was awake, and they were watching a grown-up movie. They will later tell me it is called *Margin Call* with Kevin Spacey, and there was a long section in it with this one word being used as

Slow Takes a Long Time

a noun, adjective, verb, and adverb—pretty much any way you can use a word, for the etymologists among my readers.

But it is a bad word, requisite four letters and all.

After this rock-throwing incident—well pretty much right after it—I felt like I had done something very, very bad. By the time my mother saw the e-mail about it, nearly a whole day had passed. She came rushing to the school to give me my own "early release" and take me with her to her class at a college nearby, where she teaches about things that happened long ago, things both bad and good.

She wanted to ask me what had happened.

So after I apologized for what I was not entirely sure, I told her the names of the boys who had called me "different." I truthfully told her I had picked up a rock, and I admitted saying the bad word. Then I repeated the bad word and asked her what it meant. I always try to tell the truth, and I was not sure what I had done that was so bad. "I don't want to be different," I told her.

She was very quiet, breathing in and exhaling, and a tear rolled down her cheek.

So we were driving to her class, and I was just very, very happy to be out of school early and driving with Mom. She stopped and got me a Happy Meal and a boy toy. We kept driving then walked to her class. I walked into the lecture hall, approached the podium, and said hi. The students who were there giggled. I liked that. Then I said, "I am ____"

and filled in the blank with my English name. They giggled and smiled.

With this audience, I was on a roll.

Mom began talking to her class. Oh goody, there was a piano up front, so I walked over to it and hit some keys. She looked at me and said, "Shhhhh. Be still." One of the students said jovially, "Let him speak!" The class laughed again. They seemed to like me a lot.

Thinking she should not cancel class and must keep going, Mom said some very official-sounding things.

I hit the piano keys again. I really liked the sound of them, to which she responded, "Come over here. Here, write on the board."

I started drawing. The class giggled. Then Mom started talking faster. Then, possibly carried by their energy of interest, I walked over to the piano again and hit some keys. The class giggled. Whatever I did was eminently more interesting than what she did. Of course, in retrospect, it wasn't a competition really. I just wanted to meet audience expectations.

She put in a film showing—of course, I did not really know this yet—Japanese fighters attacking mainland China prior to World War II. Later I asked her, "Why are those bad guys shooting those other guys?"

She called Daddy on her cell phone to ask breathlessly, "What are *we* going to do?"

Slow Takes a Long Time

Again, I do not know all this. I have just had a great time at Mommy's work. She was about to fall apart because I hadn't done what I was supposed to. I was a bad boy, I think, but I feel oddly good. Proud. I liked the sound of laughter. These older kids did not call me different; they thought I was entertaining. I liked the noise they made, and I seemed to have a sixth sense as to how to illicit their roar of approval.

The next semester, one of those student witnesses—a twenty-something girl from Mexico who wants to be a doctor—would ask Mom when she was going to bring me back. She was in another course with Mom and often visited during office hours. "He wants attention and knows how to get it," Mom said observantly. She had heard more about my new special-ed status and added, "I couldn't express myself when I first came to this country. *They* didn't understand. He is not retarded. I do not see that at all. He is smart. He knows what he wants."

My mother was just thinking about the psychologist's and the teachers' reports, the labels, the acronyms, and another *R* word: *respite care*.

Although I do not know this, and my parents have not expressed it to me, it has not always been easy trying to understand my needs. I am very good at reading faces—actually a Chinese tradition well before jury consultants began helping lawyers do this—and I have seen my mother frown, look sad, and cry.

One time, she was crying. It wasn't just about me; it was about other things. Her mother was dying, and her middle sister was in decline too. All I knew was that she was crying, and my father had raised his voice in frustration "about things."

I kept going back and forth to the refrigerator, filling cups with ice and water. It was all I knew to do: provide comfort or sustenance through water.

They both have been frustrated by my repeated and nonstop—sometimes up to thirty times—questions. Mostly, though, they have just been worried. It has gotten much better for a variety of reasons, maybe just my own sense of stability; and as I've grown, I recognize what I am doing.

I grin my crooked Harrison Ford smile, and everybody smiles back.

For older parents, it is sometimes easier to forget how scary things seem. They might later tell me that even normal memory loss can be blessedly numbing.

Alphabet Soup

I am not just ID. I am ADHD (attention-deficit/hyperactivity disorder), and I stutter.

I am always "wiggly," and thoughts come at me rapid-fire. I was here in the United States a year and a half before my parents sought medical—pharmaceutical—help for me.

I was in kindergarten and was having a challenge "behaving."

So after a while, my parents took me to a veteran psychiatrist. Mom and I went into the office, and I was, as they say, "bouncing off the walls." I went from one brightly colored toy to the next. I played with the doctor's lava lamp. I kept interrupting: "What's this?" "Can I play with that?" I knocked a few things over. And the doctor had the teacher complete what's called a Vanderbilt survey. I went on Ritalin.

Yep, I am ADHD.

I don't use the term, but I know how to take my pill, and my pill "calms me down." I actually feel better, although I sometimes pick at my skin on the higher doses. I will ask for the pill if I am feeling ill at ease or full of what my parents see as analogous to electrical currents pulsing through my veins.

On weekends and breaks, I take a lower dosage because the medication has also affected my weight and maybe my growth, although I am now four feet three inches tall and not much more than sixty pounds. I just know my parents talk a lot about me eating and growing. I like when ice cream is involved or a green drink at Dairy Queen, but they mix in baked chicken and green beans. I like those too.

Second, my speech teacher has talked to me about "bumpy" speech. I get caught up less at the beginning of words and have more of an echo as I am finishing them. Sometimes I just repeat the full word over and over. Everyone patiently waits for me to get to the next one. My speech teacher showed me a video and told me that "everyone stutters now and then."

She also showed me a rubber band and is working with me to stretch out my words.

"Str-e-e-e-t-c-h."

"Str-r-r…"

"E-e-e…"

"T-c-h…"

The teacher sent home a flier that said stuttering is not caused by emotional issues. I tend to stutter more when I am excited, however. Still, I try to say what I am thinking. I usually am successful at expressing my needs and wants, which means I am a successful citizen—usually immediately but definitely eventually.

My parents think the medication and the speech therapy are helping me very much, and I like my doctor and my speech teacher. I also like my dentist, who guessed that I was as many as three years younger than my papers from China said. I also like my pediatrician, who later had my hand x-rayed, the results of which indicated I am about two or three years younger than we thought. I might better understand this later, but my parents kind of view me as a CSI (crime scene investigation) mystery.

I like doctors' offices because there are so many things to explore when I am waiting. The crunch sound of the paper on the table is cool too.

So I am younger than we all thought, which explains why I was only thirty-plus pounds when my new parents came to get me, although they were told I was seven and despite me being much smaller than some of the children identified as three-year-olds.

It also could explain why I do not always keep up with my second-grade class. And maybe it explains a few more things. The grownups here are still trying to reconcile what was said about me on the papers with official stamps, dates, and seals. And now they are adding to the narrative—ID, ESL, ADHD, and a stutterer? At times, my teachers have said I am spitting at the other children. Maybe I am; maybe I'm not.

That's a mouthful, isn't it?

Find My Bliss

I enjoy playing.

For example, I like to play hide-and-go-seek at home too. My parents keep telling me I am supposed to keep where I am hiding a secret, but the way I play, I want them to know where I am—and find me. So we take turns. I tell them how long they should count while the other one hides, or I tell them where I am going to hide. If they are going into each room looking for me—under the bed, in the closet, behind the shower curtain—I will make noise so they can find me. Sometimes I will bang to make a sound; other times I will let out a shriek or laugh.

They keep telling me I am supposed to keep it a secret, that those are the official rules of the game, but I keep showing them that this is how *I* play hide-and-seek. We keep replaying the game in which I am somewhere else and they come and get me. I do not want to go too far, and I don't want them to either. I hope they understand someday. I am a very patient fellow. Meanwhile, when we play this game, I am also a very happy fellow. They always seem happy to find me, and I like to say, "Here I am!" I draw out the *m* sound in the word *am*. "Here I ammmm!" I am so happy to be here, and they seem to be happy I am too. At least I think they are.

I also love to draw. I see something—anything, anywhere—then I say, "I want to draw that."

I did a great job on dozens of white pieces of paper redrawing the robot in the movie *Hugo*. I took special care drawing the key. For obvious reasons (or at least they should be obvious to you, a "normal" person), I have a special interest in keys.

If you have ever traveled to a third- or fourth-world country, starving children have a universal signal for hunger: They use their pointer finger and point inside their mouths. Without fail. While the couple who had come to pick me up in China borrowed an English-to-Chinese translator the size of a handheld phone, they never needed it when it came to mealtime.

All I had to do was point.

Yep, they got it, and then I got it. I gained at least five pounds that first week.

Part of it was the menu at the numerous buffets in Chinese hotels catering to Western visitors; part of it was the in-room refrigerator. I quickly combined chilled M&M's with cold Coca-Cola. And these urbanites fussing over me, who deep down figured the sugar count in my recipes were sending my insulin levels sky-high, sat back and watched me at work. So having gone without sometimes, eating today is always a lot of fun.

When I first met my parents in China, we were staying at a hotel, a Holiday Inn, just days before the start of the Beijing Olympics. The uniformed staff with English name tags was very professional, and they all spoke English to bring my parents along and Chinese for me. I felt like Eloise in the grand hotel in one of my sister's favorite DVDs.

When we went to the restaurant, the buffet was a glistening feast. The young women who set it up and waited on us those first few days were so sweet and smiling and shy and giggling. They put out the cantaloupe and watermelon and yogurt and meats dutifully. And they put it all up again at least twice a day.

I would point to what I wanted and take more than I needed. It was fun to keep filling up the plates. These new parents were a different breed than the other caretakers altogether. They would smile and say indulgently, "That's okay." Then the chorus of waitresses encouraged me too.

They were an appreciative audience, and you already know I like those.

If we used the menu, I would point to what I wanted, and they would bring it. Thus began a series of pointing and receiving. It was a great game, and it made me very happy. By the time we left China, I had gained six pounds. The clothes we got at the Chinese Walmart (it wasn't really Walmart, but it reminded me of that later) were already bursting at the seams. In fact, a button popped off. My face filled out, and I got my first Buddha tummy, a sign of good fortune.

My parents would *ooh* and *ahhh* over my poops floating in the toilet, and I was proud to show them as if it were some precious gift. It reminded them of a scene in *The Last Emperor*, when the eunuchs cooed over the steaming turd delivered by the tiny boy who ruled my old country. Of course, I did not know that yet. I just knew I had pleased them—pleased myself, actually, because it was such a relief to get that thing out of me. I had never produced such results before. Being malnourished and hungry isn't conducive to such great work. And my production continued to increase.

Once we got home to America, food preparation was very fun to me too. I liked telling my parents what I wanted to eat: Taco Cabana black-bean burritos, Chef Boyardee from a can (an amazing feat), a frozen meal (still pretty amazing), pasta with pesto sauce—spicy and rough against the tongue. I also liked to help them cook, and one of Daddy's cousins got me a chef hat so I could put on the apron and help cook too. I like to watch TV cooking shows, and one taught me the word *anchovy*. I like how that sounds. In the kitchen, stirring is my favorite job. But I always keep busy, regularly tinkering with the timer, much to my mother's chagrin. I like the vibration of it against my hand and then the zip when I turn the knob.

"Son!" she fusses. "Stop triggering the ringer! How are we going to know when the food is ready!"

One time, in the kitchen where I like to help, Mom was heating up pot stickers in a covered pan, essentially Asian dumplings. It was taking so long, so I said quite earnestly, "I can *smell* the taste. I bet it *looks* delicious." Then I asked, "Are they still done yet?"

Mom immediately wrote down the quote on a Post-it note. (She's always writing down what I say, as if it were a code to decipher, my personal boy whisperer.)

When we're done eating what we prepare, I like to think of other things to eat. I do not want it to end, this ordering and preparing and doing it all over again. I like that there is always food around. I also like to postpone bedtime through this ritual. When I tell Mom I am hungry, she always gets this puppy face and says, "Ahhh." I play on her sympathies to great effect. I think she knows it, but she cannot get the image of me as that underfed orphan from those early days out of her mind. My neck was so thin it looked like a reed straining to hold up a poppy, my oversized head. My dad later would say I looked like the alien ET in some popular movie long ago. My skin was pasty and pulled like the outside of a spring roll, opaque, and my teeth seemed to jut out in contrast.

When we go to the grocery store, I like to point at food that I want. I like to see when I will get it, but often they say no. I do not understand what determines yes or no, but

I always ask. It seems foolish not to say yes more often. Did I mention how much I like the word *yes*? Someday they will understand my nothing-ventured–nothing-gained thinking. For now, they just think I am mildly irritating, a beggar never satisfied with his lot or, worse still, a spoiled American in training.

One day, I pointed to a big "oom-bit-tie." I kept saying it. I meant *cabbage*, but my mother did not understand me. Still, she bought it and decided to prepare it. She boiled some water and dashed the pale cream lettuce-like vegetable with salt.

I ate the whole thing in one sitting!

Plus, the grocery store we shop at—H-E-B—has toys too. I always ask to go look at them. I do not usually get toys, but I get to go survey and see what is there. That is fun too.

One of my first toys was a plastic gun that flashed laser lights and made noise. We got it in China. I had never had a gun. I cannot tell you now how I knew about them. My parents do not own guns or know how to use them, but I like them very much (at least toy guns), which should be no surprise to you by now. My parents and their friends think that, in that regard, I am a "typical" boy.

I sure think so.

That first gun did not come home with us, and it will be a long time before I know that airport security was the culprit. People are not allowed to bring guns, toy or otherwise, into airplanes. I did not realize it at the time, but then one of the first things I got when we came home was a Nerf gun because friends of my parents wanted to welcome me. Their daughter was in my sister's orphanage. "Please don't hate me for doing this," the lady said to my mother, "but *we got him a gun.*" She knew what she was doing as she had a son born about when his Chinese sister came home. I am still always asking for guns or swords. My parents do not understand why, but they seem to appreciate that I make good use of them.

I sometimes play pirate too, like Johnny Depp from *Pirates of the Caribbean*. The scene where young Will makes swords is so funny. During their conflict, they dance all over the stable, and I try to dance like they do in the sword fight: foot here, foot there, arm arched backward here, and jab there.

I have an old pirate Halloween costume. Since I am not growing very fast, I have been wearing it after school year-round. Some days, I emerge from my room upstairs donned in the outfit, replete with a stretchy red bandana.

"Hello, pirate," my family says.

Some days, I wear the outfit to the store with flip-flops. I am quite a sight, given my natural swagger, in search of an audience.

"Hello," these smiling strangers will say.

So drawing, eating, playing, dressing, and greeting friendly people are among my favorite things in my

American home. In that way, I am no different from most kids I know. I may be "retarded," but I know what I like, just like that pre-med student told Mom.

When it's a special occasion or when I feel like it, I like to wear a shirt and tie, like Daddy. The first time I did it, it was just because I noticed that Daddy was wearing a shirt, tie, and jacket. So I asked for all that, and we found a nice combination at Target. I wore the shirt and tie in my first-grade group photo, then individual photo, and dressed up again for my second-grade photo. Everyone told me I looked handsome, and I felt handsome and hip. Sometimes I wear the same combination for religious services. Even at this age, I feel I can make a statement—and an entrance. At church, when the pastor says we should greet one another, I make a special point to go shake hands with everyone. I like to say my name and shake very vigorously, like a sweaty, suited political candidate—tie loosened—on a campaign stop.

Except, my smile is for real.

Love in Any Language

I am klutzy, so I still use what you might call sippy cups. My parents use Tupperware cups with lids and put a straw in them so I "don't spill." The first summer after US kindergarten, I had to go to summer school at another school. It was only about three weeks, but after the first week, the janitor in the cafeteria complained to my mother, who was my ride.

"He always spills his milk. I mop it up every time."

"I am sorry," my mother said. "He is still learning about straws and containers."

"If he does it again, I do not think we should give him milk," the lady said.

"I am sorry," my mother replied. "I will talk to him."

I kept spilling the milk, but the cafeteria lady was nice about it. She brought out her big string mop and cleaned up the spill really quickly. It was like a dance. I would spill; she would clean up.

I liked to watch her make the milk on the ground disappear. It was like she was waving a magic mop like a character in Mickey Mouse's animated musical *Fantasia*.

Poof!

Poof!

Poof!

I use a fork, but I like to use my fingers still.

When I drop—or bump into—something, I say, "Oh, sorry!" I say "I'm sorry" a lot, even when my parents say, "Oh, it was just an accident."

I'm sorry.

I'm sorry.

I'm sorry.

I say it a lot, like a mantra, to make sure my family or friends are not mad at me. I often ask, "Are you mad?" "Are you happy with me?" Then I say, "Don't be mad." Maybe because of my prognosis and spills and bumping into things, I recently defined *accident*.

"An accident is when you do not do something on *perfect*," I say.

"Correct," my mother says, thinking my interpretation is more finely tuned than any she's heard. Naturally, she scribbles this phrasing down. So there are the occasional philosophical observations. Whether they are on purpose or not remains to be seen.

The following exchange occurred after I worked on a Lego garbage truck. The box contents included a tiny plastic

Slow Takes a Long Time

banana, representing, I guess, the food sometimes left in people's refuse. I, of course, cannot imagine such waste.

"Daddy," I ask, "when you married Mommy, were you a garbageman?"

Daddy, who was answering e-mails at the computer, swirled around in the chair, swelling with pride at what seemed like a great father-son bonding moment, a continuing tradition. As an only child, he was adored and had many parent-child discussions about anything and everything.

"No, son," he replied, smiling. "I wrote stories for a newspaper. I was a journalist."

The Sunday paper was sitting out, and pointing to it, I asked, "And did the newspaper go into the trash?"

Dad chuckled, as did Mom, also a former journalist, overhearing the unintentionally deflating observation of their former oh-so glamorous and meaning-filled careers. "Yes, son, as a matter of fact, it did," Dad said.

Counting the Length of a Hug

I can only count numbers to about one hundred, so one thing my parents have me do—since I do not like to hug too long—is to count the beats of a hug. Each time we hug, they have maybe ten beats. But sometimes I regress and only count to five or so before I want to let go.

Even with the women in the office at school.

I side hug—no front hugs, except at home. And I release quickly, lest I get stuck.

Sometimes I appear not to interpret or understand or hear what other people are saying. I ask, "What?"

They repeat.

"What?"

They repeat.

"What?"

If I finally get what they mean, I say, "Oh I-I-I get-t-t it," drawing out the emphasis.

There's something else about my hearing, or lack thereof. Here's a good example: I ask my sister, "When are we going to go?" Let's pretend this is a trip to the store.

"Soon, maybe five minutes."

"Where?" I ask.

"To the store! You asked when we were going to the store!"

"Oh yeah, right," I say.

Maybe I was an absentminded professor already. I don't know. But I'm really good-natured about my family's frustrations with me. "Oh yeah, right" makes for a pretty good view of life, I'd say.

In a period of a few minutes, I might say in rapid-fire succession:

"I am going to go outside to play."

"I want to watch a *Star Wars* DVD."

"I am hungry."

"What do I do now?"

"Can I go read upstairs?"

"Can a porcupine run very fast?"

"I want to play Wii downstairs."

"Have you heard about the new Chinese Lego?"

"I like Beyblades."

"Do the moon and sun sleep at night?"

"This is my sword!"

"When I grow up, I want to be a police *ocifer*."

"I would like to work at Target, but I need to know what buttons to push when people buy things."

"Can I make a tent in my room again?"

"When can I spend the night at Jeffrey's?"

"Jude is my best friend."
"Ezra is my best friend."
"I like Bella."
"I love you, Ma."
"I love you, Sister."
"I love you, Daddy."

Ratta-tat-tat—see how I pack a lot into a short period? My sister and parents do not always see links between my thoughts and words. It can seem scatterbrained to them, but it all makes sense to me.

What Mom and Dad refer to as an oral play-by-play of my brain when I am not taking my medicine seems to me like high-level conversation. I am like an ESPN sportscaster describing a game, except it's my synapses colliding. I see the talk as bonding. Why don't they understand, I wonder? Mom's always doing the talk-to-the-hand thing when I interrupt; but I still interrupt, with her hand right up there, arm extended, palm flat against my breath.

And then again, I wait.

Sometimes when I am still, they get nervous because they always expect the antithesis. I stare at them like Eddie the dog in the old television series *Frasier*. No, I've never seen the TV show, but that's what Dad is thinking.

"Uh oh, he's become Eddie," he'll say.

I'm very still, smiling mildly and tilting my head, just like a dog, thinking.

Then there's another way I understand—or don't. I ask my parents or sister a question, and they reply in the affirmative, "Yeah."

To which I ask, "Yes?"

"Yeah," they respond.

"Yes?" I ask, seeking clarification.

There is a deep breath in the reply. "*Yeah* means 'yes,'" they respond, saying my name emphatically as in, *Why aren't you listening!*

"Oh, yeah, right," I reply.

One day, I asked my parents, "Why do parents talk about the Gerber Life College Plan?"

They were speechless, and then they realized I had seen that on a television commercial. They smiled, but I never got an explanation.

Because I talk to people assuming they are following along telepathically, sometimes I am the weird kid. I don't always know what to say or how to say it; and at the start of second grade in August 2011, I sometimes would make spitting sounds, which freaked out the other children. Nothing says "run away" like inappropriate playground behavior. I often make sounds or grunts instead of syllables, but I still like greeting people at church. Somehow I know how to slip my left hand in my pocket and extend my right. I smile and say, clear as day, "Good mornin'." We're in Texas. Some of us drop the *g* at the end of a word, like former Alaska governor Sarah Palin. Some of us say *fixin'* as in, "I am fixin' to do such-and-such."

Also, now that my parents are taking me to school so I can sleep later, I do that greeting of the crossing guards. I think I'd make a good crossing guard someday. I'm assigned to younger kids at school in what they call a child's leadership program, which tries to teach me how to model official behavior. Lord knows I have been around a lot of officials.

I like authority in some ways. I mean, I haven't always trusted it; but I'm seeing its good aspects at school, at church, and even at the time a policeman stopped my mom and me on a Sunday morning. At first I got panicky and started to cry. "I don't want to go with him!" I screamed. My parents have wondered since—because of that and other comments—what exposure I might have had to law enforcement.

As it happens, all he was doing was pulling Mom over to tell her I was waving my hands out the back of the window. I was waving to everyone good-morning! Oblivious, Mom was driving us back home and was balancing some McDonald's pancakes containers on her lap, with a drink holder precariously straddling the console.

Startled by my screams, the policeman promised he wouldn't take me, and Mom was relieved. She would later tell me she had a musket replica for her class on the backseat floorboard and did not want to get arrested herself.

Sometimes a crying child is a blessing in disguise.

"He's adopted from China," she told the officer. "He is afraid."

No warning, no ticket, just a warm, "Have a good day."

There are other such incidents reminding these new parents of whence I came, like how I regularly position myself between my family and any door. I am ever vigilant. Once, at the country home of some family friends, I accidentally locked myself in their son's room. I screamed and screamed until they could unlock it with a screwdriver. I was hot and wet from tears and in complete terror, whimpering for a long time afterward. I had gone in to see his Lego statues. When I left, I vowed never to return. And I haven't.

The first time I went to the dentist, he was told of my sensitivity to sounds I don't make, including drills. I said, "Please don't hurt me." He didn't.

Early on, my parents took me to one of three local Chinese-language schools. I wouldn't sit still and kept asking to go to the bathroom on the pretense that I had to go, given how interested they clearly were in my ingestion-digestion-elimination stages. I kept looking at that fake ceiling so popular in institutional roofing and could hear the air-conditioning turning on and off, like a faraway train.

Once, they took me to the home of a Chinese-language tutor. Although I still listen to and sing with Chinese folk songs, she said I didn't appear to understand when she spoke to me in Mandarin. I understood some things, but I was ready to go home. Old associations seemed to bring back scary memories, and I hate it when I can't see the door.

Maybe it's not so weird to want to know where you are, where you're going next, and who you're going to see.

On the flip side, my memory makes me a great shopping companion. At the grocery store, I always know the list by heart. Just the other day, I whispered, "Wet wipes and Pull-Ups and pizza and Birds Eye (frozen foods)." My American brain is a cornucopia of brand names.

So I'm beginning to think that anyone who doesn't think like I do is actually possibly weird. This is my normal anyway. The rules of thumb I follow have worked so far.

When I close the door to my room, my father says, "He's going into his laboratory."

In a way, beyond trying to interpret what seem to be idiosyncrasies, my parents see me as a tinkerer who has potential to become a car mechanic or an engineer. I always say I am doing "spearmints," which they take to mean "experiments." The TV show *Man vs. Wild* taught me about *evaporation*, a big word I can say, and how to survive in the desert, although—as much as pee has played a role in my early life's narrative—I think drinking pee is gross and regularly laugh about that episode.

The show also taught me the word *vegetation*, so I am always pointing out what I think it is as we drive around town.

In my room, in the quiet, I begin—and often complete—projects. "I am working on something," I yell. ("Sumzing" is how it comes out, like a German military officer in a World War II movie). I am building something.

I look at the Lego pictures or the instructions (een-strug-zuns) from the Erector set and try to replicate those.

"Look, Ma," I say in my non-inside voice.

"Look, Da," I say, as if I'm from Ireland.

"Look! Look!" I command, never allowing any indifferent reaction.

One afternoon, when my mom had taken me to Valvoline to get her oil changed, I pressed my face toward the glass partition and watched the man underneath the car. They had stepped down below it and looked up into the engine, pondering the spaghetti of wires and coils of metal. I really wanted to be out there with the men with names on their work shirts and thick-heeled boots. I wanted to be in the heat, closer to the strong smell of oil and gas and rubber and the hum of the fans.

"I can do that," I said.

Mom nodded and then wrote down that quote on a piece of paper, marking her spot in a book she was reading. Inside, she was clinging to that thought as my professional calling, that my mechanical ability, still at Lego level, would be my salvation when she and Dad were gone. After all, everyone in this world should have a fully completed Lego structure. Everyone needs access to a car with clean oil.

Or I am trying to create a system for something. For example, just the other day, I took two air pumps and wrapped their snakelike plastic tubes around the bottom of two lamps downstairs. I called my mom and said, "See!"—my version of *eureka!*

Often, just like the robot in *Hugo*, I will see something on PBS or Nickelodeon and want to draw it: a map from *Dora* or a pineapple from *SpongeBob*. I will draw or dress up like Indiana Jones. My parents say that I draw very well, that I am a keen observer for sure.

I am a young detail man; and my parents could tell from my sketches, including that dark apartment room of my youth, that I was redrawing what I had seen. I don't know if I have a photographic memory, but it is pretty darn close.

Our refrigerator is plastered with my artwork. About six months ago, I asked my mom if she would get my artwork framed, just like my sister's.

Now, a collage of an eagle, maybe a phoenix, and some kind of colorful bird is framed in my room. I am very proud of that work. It says my American name in big white letters on a black background and "Fall 2011."

Still, as observant as I am, I do not know I am *retarded* because no one has ever said that to me. I started my story with this word because I might realize later that it stings if you accept the old definition of a very old word—and because, now that you know my story, you might also flinch any time you hear the *MR* or *ID* phrases.

I do not know I am MR or ID because, after you know my story, how could you think that I am either or both? After all, without knowing it, I live the embodiment of self-help messages, the Torah (the "law"), the Koran (the "truth"), or the Bible (the "book"). I thank God every day in my own way. No, I don't say it that way; but as soon as I know it is morning and I am in my room with my girlfriend's name on the wall and Legos all over the floor, with clean clothes and an egg and milk awaiting me, I smile again.

If you were to ask me—and I hope you do someday—I would tell you, like the buffet ladies in China who wooed me, that I am *lucky*.

I am lucky because I am loved, and I am happy. I am also lucky because I survived a whole lot in my first few years.

I know China is not a bad place. It is a rich land of brilliant achievements with fathers and mothers and sons and daughters who love one another and laugh. It just was not a good place for me. At the same time, it took several good people to get me to this good place. Someone took me from a bad situation and brought me to a better one. In their own ways, in their faces in the photo book in my little room, I see that some of them too loved me very much.

I am a child of neglect and abuse, but I am no longer either. Life isn't perfect. My life isn't perfect, but it is a whole lot better.

That is my story so far, and I hope it makes you feel a whole lot better to know it. I do not want you to feel sad. I want you to feel happy. In fact, one of my oft-repeated questions to anyone I care about is, "Are you happy?"

Are you happy?

Are you happy?

I am empathetic. When I hear another child cry, I pause and ask about him or her. When I see my parents or sister with a serious face, I ask why. When I feel sad, I ask for help. Enough good people reached out to me, grabbed my hand, and—eventually—gave me some hugs. Even now, the school office ladies do that. And they hold on tight, and they have taught me to hold on tight, to give and get "real" hugs and not feel trapped.

Even if I am not the smartest person in the world, I am smart enough to know that I am loved and safe. And that makes me smart enough.

At our local Asian restaurant, I point to another food item, "Happy Family," and I always eat the whole thing. I like the word *family*, which I say as "fam-ee-lee" with an ending echo.

That is pretty smart. Food and family.

Family.

Family.

Family.

"Fam-ee-lee."

Lessons from the Happiest Boy in the World

Maybe someday I can assert that we all have special needs. Again, I have not ever heard the term *retarded*, which is the way we children were labeled in my parents' generation. After reading an e-mail about the grim predictions for me, my mother's godfather—whom my sister and I sometimes call *Grandpa* because that's what he feels like—sagely advised my parents not to acknowledge such a label, lest they give it a negative power.

Of course, it is not in and of itself a bad word; it is descriptive: to retard or delay. It is not much different from *intellectually disabled* (ID) for that matter. My American dad prefers the word *delayed* because it suggests the potential to catch up. Throughout history, my mom will later tell me, humans change terms in an attempt at better describing their surroundings. For example, African Americans were once *Negro, people of color, black*, or now *African American.* My mother has Cherokee ancestry, Indian, now referred to as *Native American*. My father, a Hispanic, was once called *Mexican American*, *Spanish American*, or *Canary Islander*. They both share English, French, and Irish heritage; but they tend to go by *American*, which is an accurate and apt term for me.

Like the fashion designer Dana Buchman, my parents prefer the term *learning differences* to describe my set of challenges, and my teachers use *special education* to describe the combination of classes and approaches I receive.

These are different words to say the same thing. Different words that today—because of teachers and families who spend a lot of time thinking about all this—acknowledge that some things take time to get to us but eventually often do. *Retard* when used in terms such as *fire retardant* suggests protection. The more you know about retarded children, the more you can protect them.

So when it comes right down to it, and it always comes right down to it, we are all retarded or intellectually disabled in certain areas at different times of our lives. My father is terrific at statistics and algebra; my mother prefers basic math and computer calculators. My sister is terrific at reading and writing, Tae Kwon Do, golf, and archery. And I have not mastered those skills. Point of order, however, when I took Tae Kwon Do for a few weeks, I did learn to tie the white belt properly. In fact, I spent fifteen minutes of each thirty-minute lesson tying the belt. You already know that I appreciate clothes; and now that I am in Cub Scouts,

I am as meticulous about dressing in my blue-and-yellow uniform (including a neckerchief and cap) or my red-badge vest as any military man. In fact, Daddy sometimes will hum ZZ Top's "Sharp Dressed Man" to me.

Although school documents lament that I lack an understanding of place value—which includes the ability to describe "the value of whole numbers to 999" and compare and order them to 999—I diligently work on my homework. I write my American name and the date and work a few pages most nights, and then again, I read. I might not "demonstrate proficiency on most of the language arts," but I am communicating every day in a way many of you would never have to.

So we do not describe the story's plot and its elements in identical ways, but we can get to the happier endings. I do not know that I am retarded or ID. And by the time my parents sit down, all with serious faces, to illuminate me about it, I still might not know what they are talking about.

After all, if I am the happiest person in the room, I am a lucky young man, no matter where I came from or where I am headed. And there is something in my face that suggests I know my parents and teachers will begin to understand that eventually. For now, at least, they meet my needs.

A few months after my story began pouring itself into these pages, I got to ride in a golf cart with my mother, watching my father caddy for one of my sister's golf tourneys. When they introduced me to another mother and her daughter, also a player, I said, "Tell them I am an awesome boy!" And they did.

Retarded, intellectually disabled, smart enough—of all the words to describe me, I like the sound of *happy*. That's why I point to it on the restaurant menu.

A few months after arriving here, I told my new parents something musical to their ears. I had a full stomach and felt clean and was playing upstairs.

"I happy," I said.

From this vantage point, I am the happiest boy in the world.

Lessons I have Taught My Family[1]

Acknowledge when you do not understand something. I always am repeating questions or asking my parents to repeat answers until I understand. Sometimes they think I do not hear well, but I am listening and trying to learn.

Show you understand. Once I understand something, I typically say, "Oh, right."

Comfort others if they appear to be in distress. Another favorite phrase of mine is, "It's okay." I even say it to my parents.

---

1   It's possible that my family knew some of these things, but I believe it is my job as a child who cannot verbalize everything I want to, to communicate what I am thinking as best I can. Sometimes I have to wait for them to understand, but they eventually do. I am even teaching my teachers. Maybe even my school principals. Meetings, after all, cannot provide all the answers. I would say, if I could—and I certainly demonstrate this, if you look into my eyes—that children run on their own clocks. Children of challenge are not always aware that anyone is timing them.

Apologize if you have done something wrong. When I bump into someone or spill something, I always say, "I'm sorry." It helps people know you did not mean to do it. For whatever reason—most certainly because of the way I am wired—sometimes I apologize twenty times. But it's okay. It's better than not acknowledging responsibility, don't you think?

Say "I love you"— a lot. Sometimes it might seem like I say, "I love you" too much, like a windup doll, but I say it all the time. I like to hear it too. My dad and mom learned to say *Wo ai ni* or "I love you" in Mandarin. They will squeeze my hands three times as they say it, so sometimes we telegraph the message to one another through touch. When I met my new parents, it was the first time I remember hearing it. I never tire of hearing it. Usually those three words accompany another demonstration that the person saying it really feels it, so I know what love means, no matter how old I really am.

Tell people how you feel. I have no filter when it comes to expressing my needs and wants. If a stranger gets too close and I do not like it, I move away and make a face and, sometimes, even make a loud noise. Then they usually respond in the way I want them to. As long as it is the right situation to be this way, often being direct is the best way to be.

Let people know you are there. I think being quiet is overrated sometimes. Like I said, I often like to make noise.

I like to shake hands. I like to say my name. Even if they think I am "different," people at my school know who I am. Wherever we go in our neighborhood, we meet someone who knows me. You know why? Because even if my start in life was not as promising, I make sure people know I am here now. If you don't like something, communicate it somehow. Noise and the sounds you choose to make have their place.

Play along. When it doesn't hurt you to do so, play along with other children and grownups. For example, when we go to the McDonald's play area, I take turns chasing and being chased. I will meet a stranger, but after we do that for a few minutes, we are no longer strangers. I tell other children my name and ask them theirs. My parents see that as "nice" manners, but I think it is the way to make friends.

Dress appropriately. Jeans and shorts are wonderful inventions, but sometimes it is appropriate to dress with flair. I like to wear a shirt and tie, like Daddy, on special occasions like group or individual photos. I met my adoptive parents in a faded T-shirt, shorts, and girls' sandals, nothing more. I have a couple of *Star Wars* T-shirts. More recently, I like to wear my Angry Birds T-shirt. So if you can, dress for the occasion. It makes you feel proud.

Pay attention. When I was younger, I sometimes was dropped off, and the people who dropped me off did not come back. It made my insides ache. Today that does not happen anymore, but I always pay attention where we are going, just in case I ever have to find my way back. An old fairy tale, *Hansel and Gretel*, shows how children put out bread crumbs so they could find their way. I say know your surroundings, and you will never be lost again.

Know where you are and where you're going next and who you're going to see. Otherwise, you might get locked in a scary place. Knowing your surroundings and also reading faces—those two things are all you really ever need to know. Other things fall into the category of "good to know" but not as essential.

Ask nicely. I find that when I ask my sister to borrow her Wii or iPod, if I ask nicely, she usually says okay. Now, sometimes she will say no; but then, maybe because I ask nicely, she will let me borrow them the next day.

Always ask for what you want. There is a saying in my family about five minutes. Five minutes is the increment of time most often cited, as in, "I'll be there in five minutes" or "I'll give you five minutes before bed." I do not tell time exactly at this stage in life, but five minutes is a good amount of time to start with. So I always ask for five minutes and usually get more. I plan ahead and have a book by the bedside and usually can get the grownups to read to me or listen to me read. Asking for what I want is one way I have listened to and reread *Green Eggs and Ham* as much as I have. Sometimes it is important to consider how quickly porcupines run.

Say thank-you when you get something you want. I say thank-you a lot too. There are many nice people supporting me, and it feels good to thank them. I also like to be thanked and will remind my parents and family to say it if I don't hear it right after I do something nice.

Step up and get the job done. If someone else isn't doing something, do it yourself. That's the basic lesson of survival and will serve you well. After all, I walked an offering plate all the way from the balcony to the front of a church once.

Say self-affirming words to yourself or aloud. "I am an awesome boy!" is how I once described myself to strangers. They smiled in agreement. Oh, sometimes I say, "I [am] smart."

Deprivation to any degree is the only way to achieve appreciation of any degree. Okay, I have not fully formed this concept; but my sister, father, and mother believe this is why I am always smiling. In other words, appreciate, appreciate, appreciate what you have because it always could be worse. I know.

Try to tell your story no matter what words you use. We do not describe the story of our lives in identical ways, but we can have happier—even happy—endings. I use words, sounds, and facial expressions to convey exactly what I need.

Backword

Usually, writers add a foreword or afterthoughts to a book, but here's my "backword." It combines my professional tendency toward footnoting, retrospection, and looking forward. It's another way of suggesting that this is an oral history of a special-needs child getting as much support as we and his school can provide in special education.

It's a variation of how I have felt the public education system has accommodated—or otherwise—our son: backward or forward, but somewhere in between, for a variety of reasons.

This work is not intended to condemn the school administration and teachers who have labeled our son intellectually disabled or ID or, as we (and one well-meaning person at our son's school reminded me) used to say, mentally retarded. For the most part, he has received patient support and kindness. He has learned to read and write Basic English, a very different system from his native language, of which he only learned one or two characters of a minimum of three thousand he might have learned had he stayed in China. My husband and I did not teach him to read and write; his teachers did. We did not teach him the pace of schooling or the love of learning; these educators did.

However, second grade was a turning point after our son had repeated first grade and was described as *normal*. The school psychologist performed more tests (impossible-to-answer questions about his age, at times, counted against him) after the teacher reported some errant behavior. That was when our son threw a rock at some boys he later said were calling him "different." In his moment of frustration, he also said a "bad word." To her credit, his principal said, "At least he knew when to use it."

Still, after that, the special-education ball began rolling, and it was a rapid turn of events between that and the new label, one with serious implications for immediate, continued schooling. In short, he would be missing out on a portion of time in his "regular" class. Put another way, the programming designed to help more immediately—including the willingness just to "wait and see"—affect the pacing of his schooling and, therefore, his learning down the line. After all, based upon school findings, he needed special education. Beyond that, the label triggered an intense period of sadness, frustration, and fast-forwarded learning about educational bureaucracy. At different points, we were handed academic essays on special-needs education and the children in the programs. Amid the unfamiliar terms and multiple acronyms, the most validating phrase, encouraging us to ask questions as our son would, was the following:

> Frustrated parents and teachers, faced with this contradiction, often conclude falsely that such students have learning disabilities, are poorly motivated, or are just plain lazy. (*Classroom Instruction That Works with English Language Learners* by Jane Hill and Kirsten Miller)

While the "contradiction" in this case may have referred to something else, to us, it was, How could our child have gone from normal to ID in a matter of months? Certainly, there could have been a rush to categorize. Couldn't his second-language deficiency be to blame? But beyond English as a second language (ESL) instruction, these sentiments could apply to all forms of support our son was receiving, and it was an instant lesson in the experiences he likely cannot verbalize as he tries to catch up: frustration.

As a history instructor, I recognize and understand—even appreciate—the human need to categorize. Categorization is what I teach. We categorize periods of time and the people in them. We categorize their behaviors; we categorize the interpretations of those behaviors. We even categorize how peer historians have categorized as we go on categorizing.

However, what this account—or attempt to give one on behalf of our son—does seek to identify is the potential for error when it comes to our children, especially the special-needs ones. Fashion designer Dana Buchman's book about childhood differences based on her own daughters began to open my eyes, but I read that before we knew we would have a son like ours because our daughter was also struggling a bit. (She later became a strong student as it took time.) Of course, my own attempt to categorize the failure of such categorizations falls into another potential and dangerous category: the incomplete nature of such attempts. Our son's story is not complete because it is not over. He continually demonstrates a very powerful desire to survive. He has already survived quite a bit—his abandonment (or abandonments) then malnourishment and now the United States's, more specifically Texas's, education system.

Because of standardized testing, public education has narrower room for someone such as our son. In Texas, the real pressure for taking standardized exams begins in third grade, which is where our son was (or was not) heading when the mood at school began to change. At least the new label was a stopgap; meaning, he would not be penalized for his lack of performance on such exams. We are beginning to appreciate the need for what are called early interventions. At the same time, we fear what the labels they entail could mean for his continued progress.

Another challenge is that we immediately cannot afford all the services he seems to need or might need. Not trained to homeschool him, we continue to try to help him navigate by getting an education in education. If there is a hero in his story so far, he is the hero. A little Chinese American Indiana Jones, another one of his favorite characters, battling often-ridiculous obstacles. Only, our son fears hand dryers rather than snakes.

We do not blame China and know there must have been dozens of people, Good Samaritans now anonymous, who made sure our son survived and got to a better place, in no small part, due to the funding they receive from international adoption. His "bad" experiences could happen—and have happened—to children in the United States, as they can anywhere else. He happens to associate his survival and "good" things with this place he calls America and the people he calls Dad, Mom, and Sister.

Much is made about how public school teachers are overworked and underpaid. As an adjunct history instructor working long hours and earning even less than they do, I am naturally sympathetic. It is difficult for parents of special-needs children to be honest about how exhausting it is. In our case, our son continually repeats questions.

What?

What?

What?

Mind you, we love him. We adore both of our children. We appreciate the public school support system, but—after the February 2012 meeting—think it could be better, if even simply slightly more attuned. Respite care may indeed be what we need, but for a child with abandonment and attachment issues and with the remaining uncertainty about the ID diagnosis, why must we check a diagnosis box right now? Why does the line for future services have to start so early?

Millions of dollars go into public schooling each year. Could some of those dollars be shifted to go toward supporting more of those teachers who helped a child such as our son? Can this money, can all this training, go toward giving teachers permission to raise their own hands and say, "This student does not fit into any of our rubrics." Can we hold off on a categorization with such powerfully negative associations other "normal" children understand and keep going without having to fail—or sometimes separate—him? Are there other ways?

In other words, can we postpone the categorization or create a noncategory, an umbrella term such as *multiple-sensory* category, for a child with so many variables? Or how about this—*intellectually emergent*? Or maybe *multiple disabilities* or *multiple challenges*. One professional, in attempting to clarify with new phraseology later, said our son has "Pervasive Development Disorder."

Do we have to decide in second grade? Can we, for lack of a better phrase, give him another moment to show us what he so apparently is trying to show? I do not know the answers. We certainly are in the midst of asking.

Wait.

Wait.

Wait.

With his teachers' support, we have since moved him into other grades, provided him "alternative living environment" services, and no longer pressure him after he has spent hours engaged in Lego creations from online tutorials. Miniature soda machines are his latest expertise.

But wait, there's more: Could his life story help educators pace their decisions, minimizing changes for both student and parents? As I wrote this, we had our fifth meeting with our son's teachers and multiple additional e-mails. Among the teaching team are genuine heroines, professionals who are willing to try varied approaches and not give up. One of them, one of those angels on earth, said in conclusion, "I do not see a bleak future."

It was the first time in months we had heard such enthusiasm. In March 2015, in a randomly threaded conversation about NASA, our son fittingly said, upon imagining a flight to the moon or Mars, "I've really never seen real Earth."

Perhaps he, once again, is right. Neither have we, certainly the way he sees it.

Our hope and prayer is that these educators will continue to get the support they need as we can better categorize and subcategorize the needs of our children. Is it overly optimistic to hope that bureaucracy can be put in line too?

Our son has been in this country, in this state, since August 2008. We plan more visits with psychologists and neurologists as we move forward in 2012. A few observers have suggested that our son might be on the autism spectrum. At least one said genetic testing could reveal more. We hope to find out. He has been patient with us. Can we be patient with him?

Wait.

As we enter our son's next year with us, we believe in the accuracy of the diagnosis of ADHD and the need for experimenting with ESL. However, we continue to struggle with the meaning and response to ID as we try to understand it. While we have no training in the field of special education, it seems that developmental disabilities are not as clear-cut as physical ones.

To be sure, I cannot fault the person who used the term *mentally retarded* to try to help us understand his circumstances—because what she immediately helped us understand more was how she and her peers viewed our son instead of how he views the world, and she forced us to view him in a broader way. He remains a work in progress due to language challenges and other expected developmental issues related to his earlier living conditions. He cannot entirely express his worldview. Fortunately, he had—and has—no clue of the concern swirling above him. At the same time, as other students recognize his differences and perhaps verbalize them, he might. And we want him to understand his world in the gentlest environment.

The whack-a-mole intensity of this diagnosis process falls in the category of, "Why can't we make this easier for our children?" If our son was largely unaware of the tension of uncertainty, he certainly noticed parts of it from time to time. He is too observant not to, and it isn't just when Mommy cries. Our only hope is that he did not internalize it too much. One day, after a particularly intense, question-filled day, I practically pled with him, "Please, son, no more questions today, okay?" He answered in what seemed a perfectly philosophical way: "Ma, if I'd only be quiet, I wouldn't talk so much."

Very true.

So we grappled with the determination that he might be intellectually disabled or ID. It is the uncertainty of the assessment based upon incomplete information, the variables of his past, the possibility of shared symptoms from the trauma of prior physical and psychological abuse or unintentional neglect (certainly questionable education), and malnourishment. From the day we first took our son to his new American school and the administrative staff peered down at him over the counter and questioned his reported age of seven, we have provided full information about what little we knew of his past and what "interventions" we have used since. The dentist has tried to calculate his age; the pediatrician, through a hand x-ray.

To our daughter, our son is only as old as the time he's been with us. "He came here and didn't know any of the rules," she explained logically. "He's still learning the rules."

Months later, when I mused that her adopted brother "might just surprise us yet," she had more perspective for her rattled mom to write down. "I don't think we should expect a surprise. He *is* the surprise."

So there you have it. It is anyone's best guess. To us, hers sounds the wisest. For his part, he has said, in response to having to wait for the holidays, "Slow takes a long time."

We would like to believe we are doing whatever any parent could based upon the emotional and financial resources we have. We are not modern-day Annie Sullivans to an Asian Helen Keller; neither are we Jaime Escalantes for underprivileged children. There was LouAnne Johnson, the ex-Marine played by Michelle Pfeiffer, who turned her students around too. For those great teachers, at least, the outcome is known: They had success. They made a difference. They were the subjects of books and films. About all we know is that our son has bonded with us to some extent. He says "I love you" multiple times a day and smiles a lot. We cannot say what he might have been like had he been left behind in China, had I not inadvertently, really, clicked "boy" when we were trying to push our second adoption forward.

If our child is retarded or intellectually disabled, he—at least, so far—can claim to be one of the happiest boys in the world, an achievement in any circumstance. There is a theme park in South Texas called Morgan's Wonderland, created in recognition of this growing group of special-needs children, these kids who help us appreciate the wonder of life. We would not wish this uncertainty on any other child or parent. At the same time, there is this part we would like to remain precisely unchanged: his utter happiness in our world.

In his 2012 book *Father's Day: A Journey into the Mind and Heart of My Extraordinary Son*, Buzz Bissinger described such traits in his grown son—who, in so many ways, reminded me of ours—as "uncensored innocence" combined with a "valid sense of logic." We wish that too for all the other children, adopted or biological, who are on the other side of that state known as normal. And we wish their parents understanding. To this, Bissinger also spoke, "Any parent who has a child that is different has a right to be irrational. It is how we cope. It is how we pray."

Amen.

Since unwittingly beginning this book, our son has become the teacher in multiple ways. A few weeks ago, feeling overwhelmed about challenges expressed by a few of my "normal" students, and how to advise them, I asked him if he ever felt sad or frightened. I certainly have and was.

"No. Why?" he replied blandly.

Why, indeed? He has absolutely everything he needs. And so do we. We just need to be reminded of that.

From then on, my nickname for the "mentally retarded" child who came to us as Dang Guole is My Portable Buddha, a daily reminder that we have everything in this moment that we need.

Appendix

E-mail from a Special-Education Teacher on Oct. 19, 2012

I am so sorry it took me so long to get back to you regarding your last few emails. I actually started replies a few times, but never got to finishing them. I'm going to try to address everything here...

First off...I absolutely LOVE to see my students out in the community. I like for them to see me as a "normal" person, and I like to see them in a less formal setting, as well. It helps me get to know them in a way that isn't always available to me here. I feel strongly that the better I know my students, the better I am able to help them access information and teach them relevantly. So if you ever see me out in public, please do approach! Serendipitous learning is quite effective approach!

Secondly, medication. To be quite honest, I don't see much measurable difference between medicated and unmedicated days. On the few days that I know through you that he missed medication, I noted his behavior and focus to be quite appropriate. There are days also, that I am pretty sure that you did give him medication but yet he seems almost over stimulated and highly unfocused. But there is such inconsistency that I am not able to determine from my perspective what the correlation is, or if there is true benefit. Remember though, that the physical setup and expectation in my setting is much more individualized and I can adjust my approach more readily than within a general education setting. What does [redacted] say about the meds? Does he note a difference in himself? Does he have a preference?

The next thing I'd like to address is the idea of [redacted] repeating 2nd grade. I want to very clearly express to you that I believe this would NOT be a good idea. What we have learned over the last few years working with [redacted], as well as through formal testing, is that [redacted] learning pattern is not a typical one. That is not to say that he doesn't or isn't learning, quite frankly I see him blossoming in many ways. But I do see a highly inconsistent growth pattern in his skills. I realize that there is a very probable discrepancy in his actual versus his legal age. But legally, he is an 11 year old child in the third grade. If we look at him as a child closer to 8 years old, we still do not see "typical" skill levels in academic, or social, areas [redacted] has had consistent academic intervention, even considering his 2nd language acquisition status. When it was noted that he was not responding to the general approach, the RTI, or Response to Intervention, process was started. This included the small group approaches, specialist intervention, targeted instruction within the general education setting, and such. Despite these things, there was minimal growth in academics. I believe it was somewhere around this time that his actual age began to come into question, and ultimately it was decided that he would benefit from retention in 1st grade.

Unfortunately, however, progress was not gained in a way that we like to see as a result of retention, and you began to explore the idea of something else going on. Special education testing indicated that [redacted] has significant cognitive delays. I expect that hearing such a statement was a significant blow in and of itself to you. But in your omnipresent desire to do your best for your son, you accepted our offer to admit him to Special Education and give him a highly individualized academic plan. This is where I entered the picture.

I do see [redacted] as a student with significant cognitive delay. His struggles with basic math concepts and higher level comprehension are consistent with this. Under no circumstances though do I think this should impede our expectation for him to learn necessary skills. But it impacts the approach we need to take with him, and it impacts the amount of time he will require to learn those skills. The general public education system is set up in a way that will follow the developmental progress of most children. [redacted] learning pattern has already shown us that he does not follow this typical timeline. Though he is functioning at the 1st to 2nd grade level in math and reading now, there is no indication that another retention would increase his ability to learn more typically, or at a faster pace. And then there would be the issue of his age again.

Your consideration of such a move indicates to me that you, too, are not seeing growth as expected. But let me assure you of some things. The Special Education system is well-equipped to educate [redacted] and, with all of our cooperative effort and support, prepare him for a productive and fulfilled life. One of the considerations we can make for him is to specialize his instruction even more and perhaps look at a different type of setting, one that includes more real life skills instruction and approaches. In [redacted district name] we have Specialized classrooms that are fundamentally created to benefit students with cognitive delays. This is considered more "restrictive" than his current service model and not a move that should be made lightly or without careful thought. But these are classrooms that use more practical and hands on approaches, as well as community based activities, than we are able to do with him currently. In the past these specialized classrooms were perhaps a more common understanding of "special education," but with increasing standards and expectations of rigor,

Slow Takes a Long Time

there is a very high standard of academic instruction present in even the most restrictive settings.

Perhaps you and I could go and look at one of these classrooms and see if this is a direction you would like to consider as well.

I am not convinced that now is the time for such a consideration myself. I do see progress from when I first started working with [redacted], and I don't feel that we have reached a plateau. But as time goes on I also see a widening gap between his grade level expectations and his current skill level. And I do not feel it is reasonable to expect that this will reverse, or be solved by another retention. The law requires that we expose [redacted] to the grade level curriculum, which is why he comes home with moose math and participates in as much instruction as he can with Mrs. [redacted third-grade teacher's name]. But you are right, it is hard to tell what is actual understanding and what is a random guess.

But either way, it is at minimum a preview of what we want him to master. As of right now, the 2nd grade math concepts are just as hard as the 3rd for him. And regardless of the concepts, I've learned that he does fatigue quickly when he is giving us good effort, making it hard to push him too far at once. The key is slow and steady with him!

I hope I haven't overwhelmed you, or overstepped my comments. I respect the decisions you make and am glad that you are keeping us informed of your thoughts and concerns. I understand your struggle to make decisions for him. We all see those little sparks of genius in him that you do, and I know that makes it even harder to understand all the other struggles we see. Let me know how I can help.

E-Mail to Our Son's Social Worker

The e-mail below was sent to our son's former social worker, current psychiatrist, and friends immediately after the fateful meeting about test results. Each responded, and many telephoned to offer their observations and encouragement, essential to parents entering the world of special education.

Attended an assessment of [redacted] with [redacted] for an hour and a half. She was trying to explain the ID category and used the term "mentally retarded" as a way to help me understand the implications of scores showing him at 50 percent in most categories. She suggested we have him categorized as ID (intellectually *delayed*??) to get additional community support, even respite care for us. It is true that this has been the hardest thing we have ever done. It can be isolating and frustrating. We probably need to prepare more financially, with this information. We need to continue to brace emotionally.

Let me amplify on that.

One popular definition for insanity is doing the same thing over and over and expecting a different result. With a special-needs child, parents regularly do the same thing over and over and *hope* for a different result, a better result.

We love our children. They have blessed us. But we still hope for healing and wholeness, and then we feel guilty about that. As our son has revealed the worst in us, he has also shown us the best. Moments ago, he said, "Mommy, you are the best Mom in the world." He has said that to his adoptive father, too. To be sure, we do not have much competition where he is concerned. On the other hand, it stirs me to know that he does not seem to notice our errors, a gift many parents of healthy adopted or biological children rarely receive. He is happy. So we need reminders now and then on certain days. Those are the days when our bodies and minds are tired and we venture into dangerous territory of what-ifs.

We sometimes ask—in retrospect—if the Chinese government could have provided more about his development. The documents described him as "curious." The school in Henan seemed to have other-special needs children, including a young man with a huge scar on the back of his head.

Although the school psychologist was trying to be helpful, it still caused a bit (OK, major waterworks) of a cry. I was imagining him 10, 20, 30 years from now in a group home. I wondered, Will he ever marry—or be a parent himself? Can he work?

I know he's no longer your case but: A) In case there is anyway you can help other families with this range of information (it's been since May 2008, when we got the first description of him), you are welcome to share the scenario; and B) If you have additional words for us — it'd sure be comforting.

...I was so upset, but Steve and I talked, and we want to believe [redacted] has a depth traditional, American measures cannot yet see. More than one foster family (he says six moms) and places to stay (at the last "school," he says, he stayed "seven days.") Lack of nourishment. Likely physical and mental abuse. Suspicion of adults. Also, we agreed that *we might have saved his life*, which means a great deal. And we love him devotedly. It's just natural to go back and wonder how prepared we really were, as much as we said we could handle it. Of course, over time, we are handling it all, even when it hurts. And [redacted son's name] loves [redacted sister's name], and she is really becoming more supportive of him, even allowing him to play her Wii and engaging him in conversation.

Social Worker's Response

Hi,

I am so sorry that things are so difficult to cope with right now. I can understand your sadness over the latest news, and needing to cry for a while. It's hard to hear such difficult information, I am sure. I will work on contacting another family and see if there is someone who might be in a similar situation for you to talk with. I can also recommend an attachment therapist who might have some advice for you on how to manage [redacted]s more difficult behavior issues. It might also be a chance for you to have someone to vent to and get some things off your chest that are hurting your heart right now. I also have the names of traditional therapists as well.

Concerning [redacted] himself, as bleak as things seem right now, he is still young and he will continue to make progress. I feel like parenting is a one day at a time process. One day, one week, one month, or one year is not always indicative of where you will be in five years, or ten years. All we can do as parents is to work as hard as we can to help our child. We don't know exactly where we are going to end up, but we keep trying and hoping to make a difference.

When I saw [redacted] last, I saw a child who was very physically active and verbal. He needed a lot of structure and boundaries, which I remembered we talked about—and I'm sure he still does. He was so physically active that I wondered at the time if he was ADHD. I did not see anything that would have led me to believe that he was behind intellectually. But I did see plenty of evidence that he was behind in emotional maturity. Obviously the school psychologist has access to more testing materials than China would have had at the time he was referred for adoption. So It's hard to say if we could have gotten much more / different / or more accurate info from China, but I will forward your comments and insights to the main office waiting child program coordinator.

My best to you...I think the world of you and I am hoping you can keep finding things to help [redacted].

Immediate Response from a Family Friend (and Teacher)

My only immediate insight is that [redacted] is not mentally challenged. I'm around mentally challenged students all day who cannot even begin to form coherent words. [Redacted] not only can do that but learned in a very short time how to communicate effectively in another language, with a brand new family, a brand new country and brand new environment! What tests did the diagnostician base her findings on?

Sorry I just now saw this email! I will call you tomorrow evening!

E-Mail to Holistic Specialist

This is an e-mail to a holistic specialist for whom our son drew a photo of one of the places he lived in China (December 28, 2009). The subject line was "Shaken today."

I was so shaken today by [redacted son's name] look of terror and complete discomfort as you asked about that picture. I have NEVER seen him like that, and don't believe [redacted daughter's name] has, too. He didn't have tears, at first, just a pained expression and then that sort of moaning. Then he was negotiating for attention as we prepared to leave, and a few tears came. I told him after that you are trying to help him and that we won't always get Legos after our visit. It was a tough today, for sure.

Afterward, we went to Target and got him a Star Wars Lego model to build. He worked on that and stilled himself this afternoon, and then started on another Lego, one from Santa, with a firetruck. It's the quietest he's been. When Steve told him, "You did a great job," (he) smiled his broad smile and said, "Ma—I did a great job." We'll start the (holistic drops) medicine tonight.

I want to talk to him some more, about how drawing and talking about hurt can help it go away. We have told him for a year and a half that we are his forever family, but if there was more than forcing him to sleep on a pot (it probably wasn't a toilet, as there are still so many holes in the ground and chamber pots in use—even with the Olympics), he might be distrustful for some time. He just seems to feel pure shame, and we haven't admonished him for the few times he has wet. We kept plastic on the new mattress for that very reason. We offer him toddler pull-ups and he uses them with underwear. There seems to be a pride about it, but he doesn't always wet, and often will start the day by saying, "Ma—no potty in bed!"

The only thing we show frustration with is his constant movement and talking. The other day I told him I was going to put a small piece of tape on his mouth. I was wrapping presents. A few days later—last weekend, to be exact—he walked up to Steve and me WITH TAPE on his mouth. He had the cutest expression and we hugged him and said, "Awww!" He milked it.

We simply don't know how many places he lived and with how many "families" or children. He said he had some brothers, but he doesn't really offer an image of a mom or a dad. He has asked if we'll visit again, and I said, "Maybe, when you grow up," but his inquiry seems fixated on flying in a plane again. (We did last summer, to Carlsbad, Ca., and he loves transportation as it seems many boys do.) As the holidays began to get closer, he told me he got presents in China, but we doubt it; it's sort of as tho' he's filling in some blanks with some positive images. China, and his background, simply have been so impoverished. His province is so huge. He was "found" in a market at six or seven months, which suggests someone tried to keep him for a time. Most of the babies, still primarily girls, are only weeks old when discovered.

Oh, I'm prattling on. **I would like to visit again solo. I'm off next week, then resume teaching MWF, so T/TH before I have to be on this side of town at 3:15, would be best.** I'll give it a few days before we draw again. That he let me tell you what he told me signals major trust. That no one shamed him must have made an impression. Maybe he just needs more of that. His ADHD could be a combination of whatever his background was, prior malnourishment, and lingering doubts about the permanence of this situation. I read a little Freud, any way…

E-Mail from First-Grade teacher on January 7, 2011

Hi! He came back all smiles on Monday. It was so cute. I haven't seen any hitting at all, so that is good. I changed some seats early in the week and [redacted son's name] asked me to change his seat today. I moved him to a new spot.

Yes, he is getting the idea of writing a sentence. I was so happy to see it, that I sent a copy for you to see. He has continued with it during the rest of the week. I did IRI (author's note: one of many kinds of testing for speech) him today. He repeated himself very much and dropped endings off of some words (wiggle for wiggled). He should be on level E, but he missed just a few too many words. Even with missing the words he was able to get the comprehension and did a great retelling of the story. So he has fallen a bit below level for the end of this quarter, so we just need to make sure he picks up as soon as possible.

I sometimes wonder if he doesn't let you know how much he is able read. Let's arrange a conference after report cards are ready. Maybe we can get him to show off his skills without putting him on the spot or making him nervous. Sometimes he speaks so easily and at other times he has no fluency in his speech. I imagine you see the same at home.

We loved his tie for pictures. I asked if he wanted to tuck his shirt in for the picture, but he wasn't interested in that.

I have him on the tier 2 of the CHILD (author's note: an acronym for another Texas educational assessment) process (sent a brochure earlier). We may move on to tier 3. We'll meet before then. Have a great weekend!

Email from First First-Grade Teacher on December 5, 2009

[Redacted son's name] continues to have difficulties focusing in class on assignments and activities. I have not been able to have any major control or find a pattern in his inability to focus. When he is with others, they see the same behaviors I do as well. He tries to behave correctly, but is easily influenced by others and will follow almost anyone's behavior if he sees it is funny. Appropriate vs. inappropriate behaviors also coincide with growth. It may take longer for [redacted] developmentally to "grow out" of some of his undesirable behaviors due to the fact he his developmentally behind other children because of his past.

I know that medicating a child is a "last ditch effort" and I tried almost everything as well. I just know that it works really well with some children (it may be ritalin, focalin, concerta, adderal, etc). With [redacted] it is going to be trial and error as it is with any other child should you go that route.[2]

---

2   Our son began taking Ritalin about a year and a half after his arrival to this forever family. We continue to experiment with varying dosages and days (up to weeks) without it.

E-Mail from Kindergarten Teacher on April 22, 2009

You are great parents, I think you are doing everything you possibly can. [Redacted son's name] is so lucky to have a mom and dad like ya'll. I also enjoy the sweet [redacted name]; he just gets in these moods when he doesn't want to listen, like today he was throwing his library book up in the air on the way back from the library and wouldn't stop after being asked several times. So I will keep his book until tomorrow.

It sounds like fatigue might play into it. He doesn't take a nap anymore at school, I'm not sure why. I think he fights going to sleep.

Lesli Hicks

Slow Takes a Long Time

Lesli Hicks

Slow Takes a Long Time

Lesli Hicks

Slow Takes a Long Time

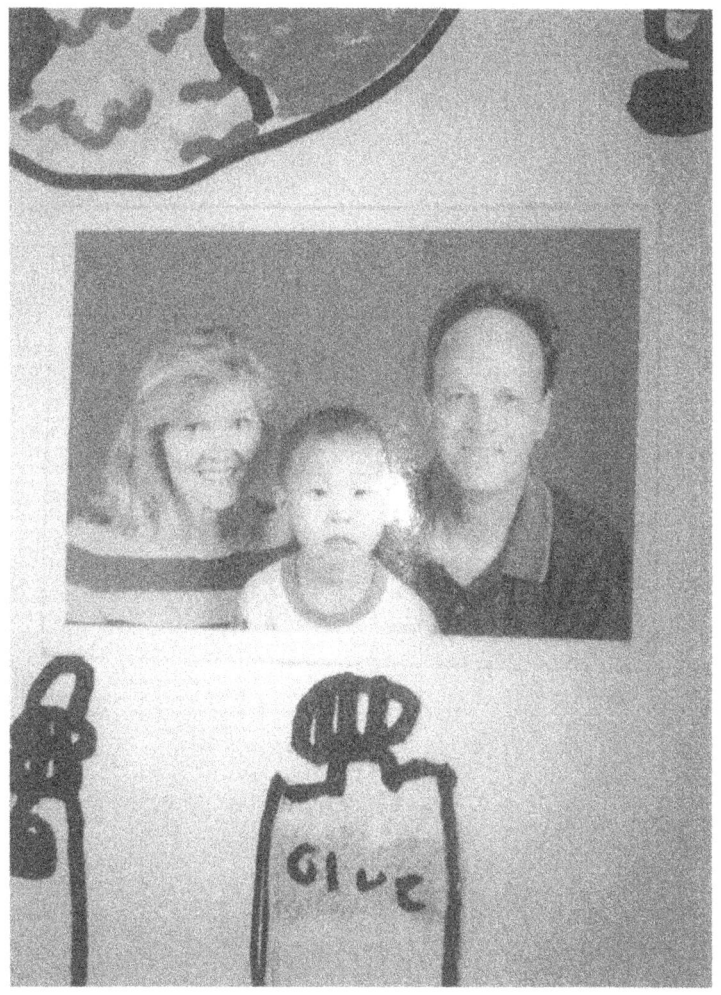

www.ingramcontent.com/pod-product-compliance
Lightning Source LLC
Chambersburg PA
CBHW070916160426
43193CB00011B/1487